Life Happens, Keep Moving Forward

A Journey Through Life's Challenges

By **Della Waggoner**, BSN, CRRN

(Retired Nurse, US Air Force Veteran)

Life Happens, Keep Moving Forward

A Journey Through Life's Challenges

★ Copyright © 2024, Fidela Waggoner. All Rights Reserved ★

No part of this publication may be reproduced, stored in a retrieval system, or transmitted in any form or by any means, electronic, mechanical, photocopying, recording, scanning, or otherwise, without the prior written permission of the author.

Limit of Liability/Disclaimer of Warranty: While the publisher and author have used their best efforts in preparing this book, they make no representations or warranties concerning the accuracy or completeness of the contents of this book, and specifically disclaim any implied warranties of merchantability or fitness for a particular purpose. No warranty may be created/extended by sales representatives or sales materials. This book is a memoir and family essay. It reflects the author's recollections, opinions, and experiences over time. Some events have been summarized and compressed, and some dialog has been reconstructed to the best recollection. No harm is intended by any comments regarding specific people written about in this publication. The publisher, author, and editing team shall not be liable for any loss of profit or any other commercial or reputational damages, including but not limited to special, incidental, consequential, personal, or other damages. Photos were all provided by the author who obtained permissions and assumes full liability for their use.

ISBN-13: 978-1-942836-45-2

Written by Della Waggoner
Editing by Janey Ranlett Editorial for Advanced Publishing Concepts
Cover design by Advanced Publishing Concepts using an original painting by Wayne Waggoner (the butterfly is explained in the book).
Book layout/formatting by Advanced Publishing Concepts

Printed in the United States of America

Published by: Advanced Publishing Concepts

(a division of Advanced Development Concepts, LLC)
141 Bogart Ct., Roseville, CA 95747 (916) 782-4272
www.AdvancedPublishingConcepts.com

This book is dedicated to
my mom, Josefa, and my son Jeremy.

Life Happens, Keep Moving Forward

Table of Contents

Dedication (p. 3)
Table of Contents (p. 5)
Prelude (p. 7)
Chapter 1 – Growing Up Poor (p. 9)
Chapter 2 – Life on the Farm (p. 35)
Chapter 3 – The "Wander" Years (p. 61)
Chapter 4 – Graduation, Now What? (p. 67)
Chapter 5 – Serving My Country (p. 73)
Chapter 6 – Reality Check (p. 89)
Chapter 7 – Return to Civilian Life (p. 103)
Chapter 8 – Love and Challenges (p. 121)
Chapter 9 – Adding to Our Family (p. 131)
Chapter 10 – Career Changes and Surviving Cancer (p. 155)
Chapter 11 – Returning Home (p. 167)
Chapter 12 – And Then the Angels Came (p. 173)
Chapter 13 – Reassuring Family is Okay (p. 179)
Chapter 14 – Continuing to Fight (p. 189)
Chapter 15 – Honoring Jeremy's Life Through His Poetry (p. 193)
Chapter 16 – "Keep Moving Forward" (p. 207)
Chapter 17 – The End or The Beginning (p. 209)
Epilogue (p. 211)

Prelude

When I tell people my story, the usual reaction is "You need to write a book." I finally listened. What is so unusual about my story? I felt like I was on a mission to accomplish something my mother, Josefa, was never able to do. She never had the luxury of going to school or the opportunity to learn something different other than being an exceptional parent. My story is also inspired by a young man who came into our lives briefly, leaving his print on every life that he touched.

"Life is always happening, Dad, you just have to keep moving forward." He spoke those words to his father once. I think it was his way of preparing us for the time when he would no longer be part of our lives. We would learn to live by those words and they would provide the title to this book. Life happens...

Chapter One
Growing Up Poor

I was born in South Texas in the fall of 1948 into a family of fourteen children. I was the fifth child born to my 25-year-old mother. Her second baby, a son, had died of pneumonia in 1943. We lived two miles out of town on an 8.5-acre farm which my father, Albino, Sr., had purchased after he and mother married in 1940. Electricity and telephone service did not exist in the area. There was no indoor plumbing, just an outhouse with two seats. A Sears catalog served us well as toilet paper. I remember looking at the dolls and other toys advertised in the catalog and wishing that Santa Claus would hear me and bring me one for Christmas. After realizing that there was no Santa Claus, it wasn't so bad using the catalog pages as toilet paper. We had the typical "Charlie Brown" Christmas tree and rarely received any Christmas gifts. My parents always made sure we received a bag of ribbon candy, an orange, an apple and pecans in the shell. I remember when I was 10, I did get a present. It was magnetic letters of the alphabet. We did not have a refrigerator to put them on and I had long outgrown the need to learn my ABCs but it was my Christmas gift from my parents, so I played with them. We learned early on that it was the thought that counted rather than the gift you received.

South Texas does not get very cold; however, when the northern wind blows, it could get very cold inside the house. There was no insulation, only unpainted sheetrock walls. I don't remember the seams between sheetrock sections having that "tape" to cover and seal. All the supplies cost money so Dad built our home as best he could to keep us safe. I remember him making hot coals in a wash tub half full of dirt and wood, using mesquite that grew wild. It quickly burned down to hot, toasty embers that he brought into the house for warmth. Can't imagine why none of us died of carbon monoxide poisoning. Life happens...

My father was an amazing man. He was a farmer and in his spare time, he built our home. As I mentioned before, there was no insulation and many times, the roof did not survive hurricanes. Our home consisted of one large bedroom where Mom, the babies, and the girls all slept. Later my two younger sisters and I would sleep in a second bedroom. My father slept on a cot in the kitchen. The living area was likely less than 800 square feet, but it was home, and we were safe there.

The boys slept in a room that was detached from the main house. Our running water consisted of a well my father had dug with the help of a friend who had well digging equipment. It had a typical windmill with a hand pump. My father added plumbing to our house by digging a trench from the well to the back of the house, piping in cold water for drinking and washing dishes.

There was a washroom near the well and he plumbed a shower into it. No hot water but it sure felt great after a long day of picking cotton. My mother would wash all our clothes in a wash tub with a typical washboard. The woman was a saint! The girls helped by hanging up the clothes which dried quickly in the hot Texas sun. Mother would also iron most of the clothes. My brothers' jeans were always nicely pressed. A heavy iron was warmed by setting it over a fire. The trick was to get it hot enough to iron clothes but not too hot that it would burn them. The built-in wooden handle kept your hand from getting burnt.

Although there were plenty of chores to do, we always had time to play outdoors, in the woods, building "forts" and climbing trees. Since we had no electricity, television did not distract us from our outdoor fun. At the time, I knew nothing different from this life. Although it was an everyday struggle to exist in a world which made survival difficult, my parents never complained. I truly believe that they were the most amazing people in my life. How they managed to raise all of us with limited funds and little to no health care is beyond me.

Mom (Josefa) and sister Marina

My mother breastfed all of us. I can't imagine the baby formula bill if she could not. She believed the old wives' tales that a woman would not be able to get pregnant while breastfeeding. She got pregnant almost as soon as the baby was eating regular food and running out in the woods with us. She delivered all her babies with the help of a midwife except for her last child. She went to the hospital when Louie was born.

He was probably the smallest in birth weight, but he was her 15th delivery. We never knew when a new baby was coming until we were all hustled into our vehicle and taken into town to our aunt's house. My father would then collect the midwife to assist with the birth and go back to the farm. I cannot imagine being my mother, in labor and left alone at the farm until my father returned. I wondered if there may have been times when the baby came before the midwife arrived. After so many pregnancies, labor must have been short.

One of my younger sisters, Marina, reminded me of the time that we all got in the car but didn't make it to town to our aunt's house. She tells the story of walking into the room when the baby was being delivered. Dad had quickly hustled her out of the room and sat with her outside the front door, just talking to her. She felt as if they developed a special bond during that incident. Later as a 16-year-old caring for Dad and the family after mom died, she proved she could manage any challenge. That is why later after mom died and I lived with them, I realized that she was really in charge. But again, we all have the same DNA and survival is the name of the game. Many times, I remember my mother going "back to work" after birthing a child. There was no six weeks maternity leave in those times. No paid time off. She truly was a saint. Besides tending to the house, she also picked cotton alongside us, and cooked for everybody when we got home. She was certainly one of a kind.

Discipline was just part of our lives. Our mother never spanked us and our father always threatened to. All he had to do was take his belt off; he did not have to use it. One of my brothers had a very difficult relationship with our father. He was quite stubborn, had some anger issues, and was the one who was disciplined the most. He continued with issues throughout his adult life and always seemed to have problems maintaining a loving relationship. He did marry twice and had two wonderful sons, but he had difficulty being a loving father. When we were children, there were times we found him inhaling gasoline fumes from the tractor or car. Apparently, it caused a hallucinating effect, and it was probably his way of "escaping" the life he was struggling with. Today, he may have been diagnosed with a mental illness. He seemed to be angry all the time. Some of his issues were also exacerbated by alcohol use.

He was my first sibling to die. Common health issues in our culture are diabetes, heart disease, and high blood pressure. The difficult life on the farm, exposure to deadly insecticides, and a diet high in carbohydrates and fats made it difficult to survive. Santiago, or Jimmy as we called him, developed heart issues and diabetes and passed away from a massive coronary at age 49. He was able to give my sister Eva away at her wedding in the summer of 1991. I think we all realized that he had some mental issues, but no one knew how to help him. He dropped out of school after 8th grade due to difficulties with learning. As a child, when he was old enough to start school, he refused to go. In fact, on his first day, he left the school shortly after the bus dropped him off and walked the two miles back to our farm. When mom asked why he did not stay at school, his response was, "I did not like their water."

Seeking medical help is sometimes difficult in our culture, especially for men. We never saw a doctor unless there was a real need. Our routine vaccines were given to us by the school nurse. We had no health insurance, so our parents took us to our family doctor's home office in the next town. He always treated us without payment or for whatever my father could give him. These were the times when people trusted each other and doctors were willing to help without payment, just because. My mother told me of a time when I was very sick and was having difficulty breathing. My parents took me to Dr. Heins, and I was given an injection which made me feel better. Apparently, I had pertussis or whooping cough and could have died. I do not remember but my mom told me I was very upset that I had received an injection on my buttocks and I let the nurse know. Interesting how later when I became a nurse, the memory came back to me. I would take great effort to be sure that my injections did not hurt or otherwise traumatize my patients. Life happens...

The smell of burning tar brings back some vivid memories. Hurricane season started about the same time as school did, in early September. If we were lucky, we just got a lot of rain and some flooding. Many times, the shingles on our house would be blown off. That's why the smell of tar is reminiscent of living through hurricanes. We would shelter in place at the elementary school in town. Sometimes, we went to relatives' homes in town depending on the severity of the storm. My mother's older brother owned a furniture store. I remember going there during Carla. He had lots of extra beds for us to sleep in. Hurricane Carla in 1961 caused the most damage. There were 46 deaths and 325 million dollars' worth of damage. In the fall of 1967, after my graduation, Hurricane Beulah arrived.

Article in the local newspaper after Beulah.

We could count on the Red Cross being there to help with food, replacement of clothing and furniture. My father always had to rebuild and replace the roof. We lost lots of pictures and other memories in the storm, but our parents always made sure we were safe.

We all had chores to do at home. My sisters and I would argue as to whose turn it was to wash dishes. There were loads of laundry to wash and iron. Housework was a never-ending job. The boys helped our father with tending to our livestock and farming our land. When the momma pigs had babies, we would all pick one as a pet, until we realized that caring for them and fattening them up only got them to market sooner. That was extra income for the family, so we reluctantly accepted the fact that they were only there temporarily. Many times, one particular pig was saved for the tamales at Christmas. These were the best! My mother made her own masa. It was perfect. Aunts and cousins would join in to make the tamales. It was an all-day affair. The camaraderie and stories told that day were all part of it. We always shared whatever we had with other families. Since we had no electricity, all foods that were not eaten had to go home with someone that had a refrigerator. The men were responsible for killing and butchering the pig. The women cooked the pork and made the tamales. The killing of the pig was a "rite of passage" for the non-Hispanic members of our family. If they did not faint, it was a good thing. Their brothers-in-law welcomed them into the family with open arms and not smelling salts. Life happens...

We also raised cattle. We kept some for fresh milk and butter, and to bear more calves for the market. The bulls had to be castrated in order for them to be fattened up for market. Did we hire a veterinarian to do that? Of course not, we could not afford that. My uncle knew how to do that dastardly deed. I remember him coming over with his little bag of tools and we wondered what was going on at the south end of the pasture. Farm life was full of adventures and experiences. This one was not high on my list of "must see."

My father seemed to know how to keep his family safe and fed. I do not remember him just having a day off. If he was not farming, he was building something or working on an automobile. As I got older and understood where babies came from, I wondered how they had the energy to make any babies and where they went for privacy. Then I remembered that every Saturday they would go on a ride into town to get groceries and sometimes they were gone for the whole day. Nine months later, a new bundle of joy would appear. It really was always a joy for us. I did not understand at the time the toll it was taking on our mother's body and health. She never complained. My parents loved each other so much.

Dad and Mom with my dog, Ackley. Old house and new house can be seen over Mom's left shoulder.

My father, Albino, with my younger brother, Abel. Abel passed away at age 48.

Our father farmed our land and hundreds of acres owned by a Caucasian lady. He was paid $25 a week for many years and eventually received a raise to $40 a week. We would get hand me downs from his boss and her daughter. My sisters and I had some nice clothes for school. Dad worked 6 days a week from dawn to dusk. Sunday was his rest day. My mother wanted him to accompany us to church but he would remark, "I do not need to go sit in a building in order to have a relationship with God. He can hear me anywhere I am. Besides, they just want your money there." I truly understood his philosophy and live by it to this day. He never liked people telling him how to practice his faith. He was a very smart man with a third-grade education.

My father on his tractor

My oldest brother, Rick. Marina, Jimmy, and Abel are in the wagon.

At the end of a long hard day, Dad would still make time to tell us stories. I remember a story about a young man who was raised by bears and was known as "Juan Oso." I admit that I cannot remember the whole story, sadly, but I remember sitting with my siblings listening intently as my father relayed the wonderful travels and good deeds of this Juan Oso character. We never tired of that story or of time shared with our father.

He planted cotton and grain sorghum but never got more than 2 bales of cotton from the 8 acres. He would alternate crops and set up an irrigation system from our well. I remember having to share that job with my brothers. The responsibility entailed sitting at the field by the pipe where the water came out so we could change the direction of flow to a different row once the water had reached the end of the previous row. It was a boring job and it was usually very hot; however, we always found ways to make life more interesting. Our neighbor grew the best watermelons, even the variety that's yellow inside. We would jump the barbed wire fence between our properties and grab a watermelon, throw it in the water for a while to cool it off and then crack it open. It was the best watermelon I have ever eaten. Sometimes we just scooped up the center of it, the part without the seeds, and gobbled it up, discarding the rest. Later we would find random watermelon plants growing in our field. Dad grew corn, which we ate and harvested to feed our cows and chickens. Depending on the season, he also grew vegetables to take to market. Broccoli grew very well. It was delicious when the flower buds were young and tender. We got in so much trouble with our father for eating the buds before they matured enough for the market. One year, he grew eggplants. No one touched those.

We raised different types of chickens. We ate the eggs as well as the chickens. We seem to always be competing with the coyotes trying to break into the coop for a tender meal or with the possums and raccoons trying to eat the eggs. It did not have to be Sunday for a chicken dinner. For some reason, I was designated as the person to not only catch the chicken but to also wring its neck once I caught it. No one else wanted to do it so I guess I was the one standing there when everyone else stepped back. It had to be a rooster, if possible, since only one of those guys is needed. It also could not be one of our best-laying chickens, so it was always a challenge. I would catch the chicken, wring its neck, and hand it to Mom, who had a large pot of boiling water ready to put it in to help pluck the feathers completely off. One day while wringing its neck, the chicken went flying across the yard and I was left holding its head. That was pretty freaky, and I refused to continue that duty. No one else wanted to do it so then our father would shoot them. This did not work too well. It killed the chicken but then we had to pick buckshot out of our meal.

My mother told us stories that her grandmother had told her about the treatment of Mexicans and Blacks when she was growing up. Her grandmother remembered walking through the woods on the way home and finding "persons hanging from the trees, decaying and oddly elongated from hanging for a while." They had been killed by the "not so lawful" Texas Rangers of that period. To verify this story, I checked the history of the Texas Rangers at this website www.TheStoryOfTexas.com. "Their story contains heroic acts of bravery, but also moments that challenge our idea of the Rangers as noble lawmen. They protected settlers and enforced laws, but also sometimes executed thieves without a trial, drove Native American tribes from their homelands, and *some Rangers even lynched Mexicans and Mexican Americans along the Texas-Mexico border."* This last statement verifies my great-grandmother's story. Yes, they were not always law-abiding. I suppose just like now, there were crooked cops back then also.

Picture from Google. Shows Texas Rangers with murdered Mexicans.

The discrimination issue has always been there. The good thing is that now there are usually more good cops than bad ones. Unfortunately, justice appears to be lopsided at times. Life happens...

These stories only spurred my imagination. Since we had no electricity, television was not a luxury we enjoyed. We had a family in town who had electricity, a refrigerator and a television. We would visit on Saturdays so that my father and uncle could watch the football game. If we stayed through the evening, we might be able to watch two of their favorite shows, Gunsmoke and Wanted: Dead or Alive. I enjoyed The Ed Sullivan Show and Red Skelton. Comedy seemed to make your troubles disappear. Television provided my first glimpse of the world outside our little town. I longed to experience more of that world. Those occasional glimpses of life outside our sheltered lives just kept me wanting to go out and explore the mysteries out there. I was excited to start school, but apprehensive because I could not speak English. Our first language is Spanish and that was what we spoke on a daily basis. Our father understood English and spoke it with his employer; however, our mother could only speak Spanish. Their main goal was working hard and providing for the family. They were a pair of unselfish, loving and committed parents who did whatever it took to make a good life for their family. At times it was disappointing when I brought home a straight-A report card and no one seemed impressed. I did not understand it then, but I realize now that my parents were just trying to survive in a life that was so very challenging. They made a commitment to each other and their children and they kept that promise: till death do us part. Sometimes it is difficult to realize the quality of parenting your parents gave you until you are taxed with the same job. I was blessed to have their DNA. I am very sure that I would not be able to deal with the challenges of life had I not had a pair of great role models.

I was torn between staying in South Texas or doing what I wanted to do. What was it that I wanted to do? The little town of Sebastian was so comfortable and safe. There were no street signs or stop lights. Everyone went to the post office to pick up their mail. It was one of those places "where everybody knows your name." Likely because we were all related in some way or another. The town was originally part of the San Juan de Carricatos land grant and was renamed from Stillman Town Tract to Sebastian in 1906. The population when I left was about 300; today it's 1,864. Hispanics or Latinos comprise 95.5% of the population. These were my roots but somehow, I had to get the courage to pull those roots up and go find the person inside who was trying so hard to get out and see the rest of the world.

Downtown Lyford. The school was across the street and over the tracks, two to three blocks down.

There were several small family-owned stores in Sebastian and Lyford. Most of the storekeepers were good about providing credit for the families in town. My oldest sister worked at one of those stores in Sebastian. Sometimes her salary paid for groceries we had purchased on credit during the week. Other mom and pop stores in the area provided the same "credit." In Lyford, there was Archer's. We went to school with their kids and one of my younger sisters married their youngest son. The small businesses depended on the farmers just like the farmers depended on them. The cotton gins and grain elevators were part of the landscape. Nowadays, they have been replaced by windmills.

Sometimes on a Saturday afternoon, our father would take us to the movie theater, where we enjoyed watching a comedian from Mexico named Cantinflas.

He was similar to the USA's Jerry Lewis. We got popcorn, shared a soda and laughed and laughed. Mom was likely at the five and dime next door with a baby on her hip and one in tow. After this outing we all packed back into the station wagon or pickup truck and made our way home to the farm, each of us holding a little brother or sister in our laps. No seatbelts back then. But again, we were packed in there like sardines; if we did crash, no one was moving!

My father and brothers visited the barber shop in town all the time. I think Dad went there sometimes just to hang out with the guys. The railroad track was a few yards to the left of the building and the post office was just to the right. The train would slow down enough for the railroad staff to throw out the bag of mail as they went by. The postmaster would pick it up and distribute it to the citizens in their post office boxes. No rural delivery then. Our father told us of a time when there was a train accident in town. I don't remember the details other than he and his friends helped pick up body parts of passengers who were killed.

The Sebastian Barber Shop, Sebastian, Texas.

This incident was difficult for him to speak about, but it was the reality of life.

Both my parents were born in South Texas and came from farming families. I never met my father's parents. My grandmother died of breast cancer and my grandfather likely died of heart disease. Dad was a young teen when his father died and late twenties when his mother died. I do remember my maternal grandfather, Felipe Perez. Unfortunately, he died when I was 4 years old. I remember going to see him in town, where he and his wife Manuela lived with one of their sons. He would sit in his rocking chair and hook his cane around our necks and gently pull us towards him. When we got there, he would put a nickel in our hand. That would buy us a Coca Cola or five pieces of one cent candy. Manuela was the only grandparent I knew for a while until we lost her in 1973, a year before my mother passed. By then I had returned to California after living in Houston for one year. I regret not going to her funeral. I cherish the memories I have of her visiting us at our farm and me visiting them in Kingsville.

Trauma seems to engrain certain memories in your brain. Although I was fairly young when they occurred, I remember certain significant events. I am not sure how old my maternal grandparents were but their youngest child, Ramon, still lived with them. I must have been 3 years old, as my oldest sister confirmed that this event happened. She could not believe that I remembered it, but the trauma singed the experience into my mind forever. While visiting our grandparents, our Uncle Ramon took us on a hike up the hill through the woods. Not an unusual event, other than someone forgot to put my shoes on. We had not gone very far up the trail before I let out a blood curdling scream and started crying immediately. My oldest sister came running back to see why. I had stepped into a pile of stickers known as "toritos," little bulls. As the name implies, they are shaped like a Texas longhorn steer head and usually draw blood. The botanical name is Tribulus Terrestris and it's also known as goat's head burr. The plant is very deceiving until you realize that you have stepped into a pile of "stickers." The entire bottoms of my feet were covered with them. That is all

I remember. My sister carried me back to grandma's house.

Another very distressing event occurred on a visit to our grandparents. In order to visit Felipe and Manuela in Kingsville, we had to go through a border patrol check. The border patrol took Mom into their office, questioning her birth certificate due to a discrepancy on the date of birth. It appeared that someone had tried to change the date. She was in the Border Patrol office for what seemed forever until all the kids started crying. Dad went in to see what the issue was. Remember that my mother could not speak English, making the officers more suspicious that she might not be in the country legally. The discrepancy was identified, and her correct date and place of birth were confirmed. This was just another example of indigenous people having to prove their right to live in our homeland.

That Border Patrol area is still there today although it has been upgraded. Everyone has to stop there, and the agents will ask if you are an American citizen. We all answer "yes" and they wave us through. One concern today is the flow of drugs from Mexico to the United States, and drug sniffing dogs are part of the team. However, there are always ways of coming across undetected. As long as people seek work or asylum from a deadly government or drug cartel, there will be a stream of people seeking "a better life in America."

Unfortunately, our politicians are so busy fighting each other for political gain, they can't figure out how to work together to manage this issue for the better.

Grandma Manuela Perez and her four sons: Uncle Chano, Uncle Arturo, Uncle Ramon, and Uncle Samuel

Uncle Frederico, Aunt Isabel, and Dad

My uncle Frederico was married to Dad's sister Anselma (not pictured). Aunt Isabel was my dad's older sister and was married to Uncle Frederico's brother, Juan. Therefore, all my cousins from both families were Salinas/Olivarez. Life happens...

Chapter Two
Life on the Farm

I could not speak English until I went to school at the age of 6. I was so afraid that I would not be able to let my teacher know if I had to go to the bathroom. My older sister instructed me to raise my hand and say, "May I be excused?" Those were literally the first English words I could speak. I was not sure what they meant but I knew that it would get me to the bathroom before it was too late.

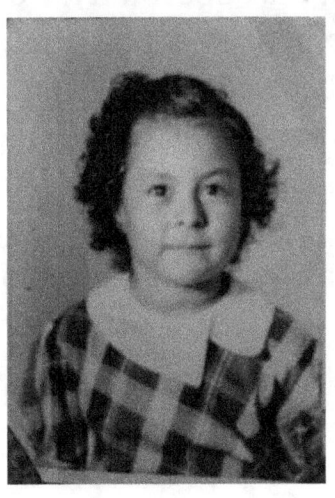

First grade

Second grade

All Hispanic children started school in beginners, now known as kindergarten. This was because English was a second language to us and we were already a year behind since all Anglo-American kids started in first grade. I quickly learned the language and was sent to first grade before the school year was over. At the beginning of my senior year, I took one of my younger sisters to register for first grade. The principal wanted to start her in beginners even though she was able to speak and understand English, knew the alphabet and could count to 100. He was the same principal who had started me in beginners, ten years earlier. I argued that she should start in first grade and if she could not make it, then he could send her back. He reluctantly agreed. She turned out to be an excellent student all throughout school and graduated with honors. I think this was the beginning of my persistent fight for the underdog. I believe that given the opportunity, we can all soar to our highest accomplishments. I was not going to let our brown skin be used as an obstacle to achieving our greatest potential. No one was going to tell me what I could not do. I knew where I came from and I was almost sure I knew where I was going. I just had to wait until I got a sign as to exactly where to go. Life happens…

All dressed up and ready for school. Me, sister Mary, sister Esmeralda, and brother Rick. To my right in the doorway, a small child is "photobombing." There was always a baby around.

Our mother always packed us a lunch, usually a bean burrito on a homemade tortilla. Sometimes if we had baloney or peanut butter, that went into the tortilla. At the time, I was ashamed of my lunch and would eat it while hiding it in the paper sack. The kids who had more or lived in towns where electricity was available would have sandwiches on white bread. Some of them even had a lunch box, and others ate in the cafeteria. There were no free lunches for the underprivileged back then. When I was in sixth grade, I was able to work in the cafeteria and received a "free" lunch. There are times when I wonder why I felt ashamed of my delicious homemade burrito. Nowadays, folks would gladly exchange their peanut butter sandwich for my burrito. I might just keep it and let them watch me eat it outside of the bag! Life happens…

Mother carrying baby Benny, brother Abel holding a fishing pole, Eva in front, and brother Fidel to her left.

Traditionally in Hispanic families, the girls would not attend school, especially in a farm or ranch family like my mother's family. Their job was to help at home with the usual womanly chores. The boys were allowed to go to school unless the family needed them at home. Going to school meant walking there since there was no school bus, another reason the girls did not attend. By the time we started going to school, there was bus service, unless it rained; then our father would take us into town. Since there were at least 6-8 siblings going to school at one time, we were in different grades. The school for "beginners" to sixth grade was in our little hometown but for junior high and high school, we had to take another bus into the next town. So, if we missed that bus, our father would drive us to the next town also. The man was a saint and unfortunately, I did not realize it at the time. If we were moving too slow, he would threaten to leave us and let us walk to school. He never did. He seemed to get things done just by threatening without having to follow through. Although I do remember one incident when one of my younger sisters would not quit crying. That was not an unusual occurrence since there were so many of us and we were always packed into a sedan, pickup truck, or station wagon. This time it was a truck, and she was sitting in the back, right behind Dad. I remember him telling her that if she did not stop crying, he was going to stop and let her off. Nevertheless, she did not stop crying and he stopped, picked her up, and sat her on the side of the road. Then we started driving down the road. We were so surprised, but of course, we did go back to get her. We all understood that he was serious when he said to stop crying! We all survived the event and no one had to call Child Protective Services. I am sure that my sister was not scarred for life. One might say that he walked softly but carried a big stick that he usually did not have to use.

Going to junior high required participation in physical education. This meant that we had to dress out, participate in physical activities and then take a shower. My sister Ema absolutely was not going to be taking showers with other girls. She chose to stay home and help our mother care for the home and the kids. Our parents did not argue, no doubt glad to have an extra pair of hands to help. Apparently, there was no truant officer wondering why one of the Olivarez kids wasn't in school. I believe there were so many of us going to school at one time that they did not realize that one was missing.

My older brother had a learning disability and difficulty keeping up with other students. Eventually, when I caught up to him in school and passed him, he quit. There were no special education programs then or at least no one to ask why Rick had difficulty learning. All but four of the fourteen children graduated from high school and four of us earned college degrees. The boys who worked as farmers during their school years seemed to have issues with learning and eventually medical problems. I am sure it had to do with poor working conditions. They handled insecticides without any safety equipment. No surprise that cancer and other health issues developed later in their lives. Rick had colon cancer and passed away just before his 71st birthday.

My sister Ema, who refused to go to junior high, became the best upholsterer in the area. She eventually obtained her GED and attended a trade school where she met her husband, Pete. She was deed gifted the family's 8.5 acres of land and home. She was always there to help our parents and continues to carry on our family legacy. Ema and her husband had three children, and two of them still live at the farm with her and their families. She also helped our older sister with childcare when they lived in Houston. She has always been a caring, giving person like our momma. She was destined to carry on the tradition at the farm. It is still the place called "home" and where we gather when there is a family reunion.

The mesquite tree in front of the house served as an outdoor service area. It was also a great play area. I remember climbing it many times and eating the sweet mesquite pods off of it. Dad would also use it to do general maintenance on his truck or family car. He would hang a pulley off one of the sturdy tree limbs, and pull the engine out if need be. My brothers were always there to help. All were jacks of all trades, farmers, carpenters, and mechanics. My dad taught them well.

Old mesquite tree then...

Old mesquite tree now. My sister Ema's grandkids play on it now.

In 1967, we got electricity to the old house. My parents' first purchases were a refrigerator, a washing machine with an agitator and wringer, and last, but certainly not least, a television set. My mother loved to watch soap operas, especially "As the World Turns," one of the most popular soaps at the time. She quickly picked up the language and at least could follow the story. She used to call this program "La Lisa" due to the main character of the show. She was able to speak some English but chose not to because she was embarrassed. She understood everything we said if we spoke to her in English. She later was able to print her name.

Throughout history, people have immigrated to other countries to build better lives for their families or to escape a corrupt government. We often saw families making their way across the back of our property on their way North where the work was. Sometimes the men came to our door and asked for food and water. My mother was always willing to share from what little we had, but my father did not trust "wetbacks" as he used to call those folks. I never quite understood that or why he disliked them so much. After all, they were from Mexico, as were our ancestors. I suppose there was a certain pride about being a "Mexican American" and not just a "Mexican."

During the cotton season, families from Mexico would come to work on the land my father farmed for Mrs. H. At the end of the season, they would return home to

Mexico with income earned picking cotton. My younger siblings and I would play with the children who came with these families. One summer, a Black family came and picked cotton alongside us. I noticed that one of the girls had an extra pinky finger on each hand, just dangling from the side of her regular pinky fingers. I was so intrigued as to why she had two extra little pinkies. But we were only about 5, so it was not something we dwelled on. At the end of the day, they would come in from picking cotton all day and sleep on the dirt floor in the building where our father kept his tools. I always wondered how they could sleep on the dirt floor in the high-humidity heat of South Texas. But one does what one must do in order to provide for the family.

Summer was an opportunity for extra money in the family's piggy bank to help with expenses for the rest of the year. My brother and I competed with each other when we picked cotton. We wanted to be faster, to pick the most pounds at the end of the day, thereby making more money. He usually won but there were times when I did. Either way, I did not like picking cotton so I was glad that some summers I was able to work elsewhere. Picking cotton was not only hard work but it was not much fun. Well, maybe that's not entirely true. We made our own fun. One time we were out in the fields and saw Border Patrol planes flying overhead, looking for illegals. We all thought it would be interesting to run and try and hide. It was pretty funny until the Border Patrol van showed up at our field, asking our father about the illegals he had hiding in the cotton field. Needless to say, our father was not very happy with us. I believe that if he had not needed to get the crop in for the day, he would have let the officers take us away as punishment. We were just making a bad day of hot humid work into something more interesting.

Robert Montalvo's family picking cotton with equipment similar to what we used. Note the woman wearing a garsole.

I will always remember that "all-encompassing, energy-draining, unable to move another inch" feeling one has after picking cotton all day in the hot Texas sun. Sometimes, when I am extremely exhausted, physically or emotionally, I will say "I feel like I've been picking cotton all day."

Dad, brother Rick, and me in a cotton field in front of our house.

Most kids look forward to summer vacation. That's the time when you are out of school and get to go swimming, to parties with your friends, to movies, and maybe get a Coca-Cola at the local mom-and-pop store. But summer vacation at our home started out by selecting a new canvas sack that could hold at least 100 pounds of cotton. Our summer was spent weeding, thinning, and later picking cotton. Our father would be sure we did the best we could and had plenty of water to drink as we filled up the trailers every day with pounds of cotton. Mother would make us headgear for protection from the hot blistering sun of South Texas. These head coverings are called garsoles. Sometimes we picked tomatoes for cash. Our neighbors who lived close to the levee were farmers and owned acreage. When their tomato crop came in, we would help with the harvesting. I did not mind that because we could eat some of the produce as we picked it. Since we lived out in the country, we had few neighbors. The two I remember the most were the Ramirez and the Guerrero families. They lived on the next farm over on either side of us. We would walk through the fields or woods to get to their homes. They also had lots of children who went to school with us and played with us on weekends.

Farm accidents were not too unusual back then as there were no real safety measures. Those were things mothers worried about then. Unfortunately, there were accidents and kids were lost. The cotton gin was a great job source but could be a deadly adventure if you were not very careful. There were no OSHA regulations back then or if there were, child labor was not part of it.

I remember hearing that one of the Ramirez boys had been killed in a tractor accident on the farm. He was best friends with one of my younger brothers. It was so sad and I don't think my brother has really gotten over it. They were 12 or 13 years old and were not only neighbors and friends who played together all the time but also classmates. My heart always hurts for the parents, especially his mother. As a girl I could not imagine the unbearable pain of losing your son. I would learn about that pain in the future.

Brother Rick, me, and Mary in between.

At the end of a long hot day of picking cotton, we would come home, shower in the makeshift shower our father had built for us, then lay on the soft cotton in the trailer, waiting to be taken to the cotton gin in the morning. We would try to count the millions of stars we could see in the sky. The constellations seemed so clear with no artificial lights to detract from them. When we went indoors to sleep, the kerosene lamp was the only light until I blew the flame out. Did I mention that it was South Texas? Humidity is just something you get used to. Sharing a bed with your sisters is bad enough but when you are literally stuck together, it is difficult to sleep comfortably. But I suppose the term "will stick with you through thick and thin" can easily refer to the kinship and camaraderie that comes from being sisters raised in the Valley of South Texas.

I learned to make tortillas by mixing pounds of flour, baking powder, salt, and lard with warm water, rolling them out for the large group of hungry cotton pickers coming in for lunch. I would make enough for at least 15 to 20 people. Sometimes I stayed home and cooked for everyone instead of picking cotton. I realized later that I would do just about anything to get out of picking cotton. As it turned out, I even joined the Air Force to get out of it. For a long time after I left home, I tried to make tortillas for myself but couldn't. There was no recipe for just four or five tortillas. My scientific experiment began and I tested them on my Air Force friends. Being Caucasians, they did not know any better and thought they were delicious. They were more like frisbees in the beginning. I had never measured anything because my mother never did. Eventually, it all fell into place. I never get any complaints. I cannot make corn tortillas, which was a specialty for Mom. Many times, I remember running home from the bus stop at our farm, as fast as I could with my younger sisters trying hard to keep up. The goal was, "La tortilla en el comal es mia!" That meant that if I got there first, the delicious corn tortilla on the hot griddle was mine. I ran track in school and was extremely fast. Homemade butter from our milk cows went perfectly with it.

Sisters and cousins at our farm in 1950s

My mother is in the center of the picture, holding baby Virginia. On her right elbow is Rick, my older brother, and I am to his left. My two older sisters, Mary and Esmeralda, are to my left, respectively. The other kids are cousins and their maternal cousins.

We had cousins who lived in the next town over and had indoor plumbing and electricity. They came over to play outdoors and we went to their house to watch television and use their toilet. During this time families were generally large. Operating a farm or ranch and managing crops took more than a village. Needless to say, we had many cousins to play with. I might say that we were never bored. If we were not playing, it was because we were working. This helped me develop a good work ethic. Life was not easy. You get out of life what you put into it. Surviving in a world that always wanted to keep me down was only going to make me stronger.

I kept the dream alive with my imagination and curiosity about what was in that world beyond the farm. Reading was a great way to escape and fuel my imagination.

Esmeralda and me. The shadow is likely my second oldest sister, Mary. The building behind is where Dad kept farm equipment.

My older sister Esmeralda could drive a tractor and helped dad plow the fields until boys came along. I always admired her for that. Because she was the first born, she filled in as Dad's helper and did a great job. After she graduated from high school, she attended nursing school at a local hospital. She is the other nurse in the family. I have always had a great admiration for her, and it continues as she is now in her 80s and is the matriarch of the family. My second sister, Mary, made us dolls and doll clothes from leftover material that mom had used to make our dresses. She became a great seamstress and baker. She is so talented that she can look at a picture of a garment and make it by measuring the client and making her own pattern. I always thought that she would have made a great costume designer in Hollywood. Four of my sisters are educators. Virginia is a paraprofessional who has helped thousands of kids navigate through early education when English is their second language. Marina, Eva, and Dorie all taught in the school system for years. The two boys remaining, Fidel and Benny, used the skills Dad taught them throughout life to become great mechanics and creators. When I was growing up, I sometimes wished there were not so many of us. Now, I realize that our greatest gift in life is our family, and I was so lucky to have such a large one.

Flour came in 25-pound sacks made of printed material. Since our main staple was flour tortillas, we went through lots of sacks of flour. Mom would try to match the material every week if she needed more than one yard to make a garment. She could make a nice jumper for any one of her babies with one yard but needed more material for a dress or shirt for older siblings. She had an old Singer sewing machine with a foot pedal that made it go. Almost all my sisters sew extremely well, but I never mastered the skill. The essential piece of sewing equipment for me was the seam ripper. My home economics teachers in high school were quite frustrated with my lack of talent, since they had taught my two older sisters. I guess they did not realize that I was on a different life path and sewing was not on that path.

Some summers I was able to work outside the home instead of picking cotton. This was great for me. I worked at the bus station one summer selling tickets to wherever anyone wanted to go. That only fueled my imagination more. Where were these folks going and what was it like there? One summer, I worked for a family-owned snow cone and fruit stand business. I became fairly proficient at making snow cones, plus slightly heavier in weight than when I started. During my sophomore year, I lived with my married older sister and attended high school in her town. That summer, I worked for a local grocery store owner. He had a structure in his parking lot with equipment to make hot dogs and cotton candy and serve sodas. I needed a summer job, so I was in. When I say "in" I mean, the only way into this structure was through the little window where the interaction with customers occurs, or so I thought. There was an area where the soda equipment came in and out so I'm not sure why I had to crawl through the window. Needless to say, I had to maintain my weight or I would have been stuck inside.

Every summer and halfway through cotton picking season, we would all pack into the automobile and head into a town that I thought was so far away. It was fifteen miles. At the Penney's store, we each picked two new dresses to lay away for the new school year. We always got hand-me-downs from our older sisters, so we made sure we liked their selections too. The boys got new blue jeans and shirts. Of course, our mother would also make a lot of our clothes throughout the year. When we were younger and not allowed to go into the store, our father would watch us while we waited in our automobile next to the lumber yard. Next to the lumber yard was what we now know as a food truck; however, this one was stationary. It was owned by a Black family that cooked the best barbeque in the whole world. Dad would buy us some and we would sit in the car in the hot sun and eat that delicious meal. To this day, I have never had anything that delicious. For a long time, I believed that Black folks were the only ones who knew how to barbeque a brisket. I still do, as nothing yet has matched that flavor. I do not remember their names or the name of their business, but I still can almost taste that delicious brisket as the juicy sauce streamed down from the sides of my mouth. Delightful!

Hunting Easter eggs with Mom and siblings

One of the best times during my childhood was in the spring. We were raised Catholic so we experienced everything that went along with that. I attended catechism classes in order to make my first communion. I learned how to pray the rosary beads and we attended the dances put on by the CYO (Catholic Youth Organization) group. We celebrated not only the religious part of it but also enjoyed hiding Easter eggs. Sometimes we just hid them on our farm. There was plenty of room there, but the best time was when we drove out of town, usually towards Austin, the capital of Texas. Mother would pack baloney sandwiches, Coca-Cola, and chips. Of course, we would have our baskets with candies and the colored eggs we brought. The Department of Public Safety Texas provides picnic tables along state highways throughout the state. In the spring, the wild bluebonnets are in bloom, and after setting up on one of the picnic tables, we ventured out to find the perfect spot to hide our eggs. The older kids would hide them and the younger would hunt. We always counted the number of dozens we hid. Invariably, there would be one egg we never found. My mom used to say, "Se lo llevó el diablo" or "The devil took it," from another old wives' tale that he always takes one.

Life was a struggle, but we did not know it. That was our life and we did not know any different. As I grew and learned in school about other places in the world, I started to question what my future held. I also realized that if I did not change the course of my life, I would eventually regret it. High school graduation was approaching, that important time when decisions are made that could affect your entire future. It was time for me to make a decision about what to do with the rest of my life.

I was fairly introverted in high school, and my two best friends were worse than me. One might say that we were "the silent trio." I always enjoyed school. I guess because it was the one place I could go and flush a toilet and wash my hands in a sink with hot water. It was the sixties and life seemed so much more interesting outside of the "Valley." My imagination was out of control. College was a non-existent thought. What's next?

I knew that I wanted to leave the area, but I was not sure how I was going to do that. Part of me was excited to see what was out there in the world, and part was extremely apprehensive about venturing out. Was I ready to enter a world I did not know or understand? There was also the part of me who respected my parents and was torn between my obligations at home and my desire to see the world outside of my comfort zone. I knew that if I did not make myself follow through with my plans, I would certainly regret it someday. Graduation had to be the beginning of the rest of my life.

My graduation picture. I was so proud of those gold ropes that identified me as an honor graduate.

As graduation day approached, my head kept filling up with questions but no answers. I had to overcome my apprehension and fear of the unknown in order to move forward. Procrastination was no longer an option. I had to make a decision or I would never know what I was capable of and what my contribution to humanity was going to be.

And so, it began. My brain was on overdrive. I had to devise a plan to figure out how to leave the comforts of home to enter the great unknown. The challenge had begun. Life happens…

Since I had graduated with honors, a scholarship may have been an option but was never offered. Prejudice was very subtle during that time. Although the majority of the population was Hispanic, I felt there was an underlying tone of prejudice towards us. I remember the day I was called to the office to speak with the principal. I went with butterflies in my stomach, wondering what I had done wrong. I had never been called to the office for anything. I walked in and he was sitting at his desk, looking at a piece of paper in front of him. "Yes sir, did you want to see me?" Without ever looking up at me, he stated, "It is my responsibility to tell you that you are one of our honor graduates." I could not be sure, but I think I may have heard him utter a "congratulations" afterwards, followed by silence. "Okay, thank you, sir." I turned and walked out, not sure if I was supposed to be proud or what. When I got home, I told my parents, who were happy and likely proud of me, but no one said it. Life happens…

Chapter Three
The "Wander" Years

During freshman year, students took "achievement tests," as they were called then. The tests included the three basic subjects: reading and comprehension, grammar, and mathematics. Math was never my strong point, but English and grammar were a different story. I learned from the best, my fifth-grade teacher, Mrs. Lokey. Dangling participles, verb conjugation, diagramming a sentence to determine where the adverb or adjective goes; all this was very interesting to me. My freshman English teacher at Lyford High called me to his desk after the achievement test results had arrived. His comment to me was, "I did not realize how smart you were in grammar and comprehension." He showed me my grades and they were outstanding. I said thank you and walked back to my desk. Years later, I wondered why he said that. Was it because I was Hispanic that he did not think I was "smart," or because I was a girl? Or a Hispanic girl! Maybe it was supposed to be a compliment, but if so, why did it not feel like one? I got angry but I also realized that things like that happened all the time and we just accepted it. Nowadays, we stand up and march about it. However, at times, we get the "go back to your country" attitude from people whose ancestors came here from Europe or England. I have a standard answer I give when people realize I am Hispanic and ask when I came to this country. "My family did not come here from Mexico; in some cases, the United States came to them."

Bear with me while I provide some Texas history. The Mexican-American War, between the United States and Mexico, started in April 1846 due to the 1845 annexation of Texas. The dispute was over the boundary between the two countries. The Mexicans believed the Texas territory ended at the Nueces River and the United States believed it to be at the Rio Grande River. By February 1848, the US had won the war, acquiring more than 500,000 square miles of Mexican territory, extending westward to the Pacific Ocean. Areas in New Mexico, Arizona, and lower California were affected. The question of when I or my ancestors came to Texas can be answered like this. My paternal great-grandfather and great-grandmother were born in 1842 and 1846 respectively, so they were just babies on the south side of the Nueces River when that decision was made. Hence, my response was, "My great-grandparents went to sleep in northern Mexico and woke up in Southern Texas." Not literally but almost. Unfortunately, even today, some descendants of European and English immigrants continue to insist that this is their country. Life happens…

Life Happens, Keep Moving Forward

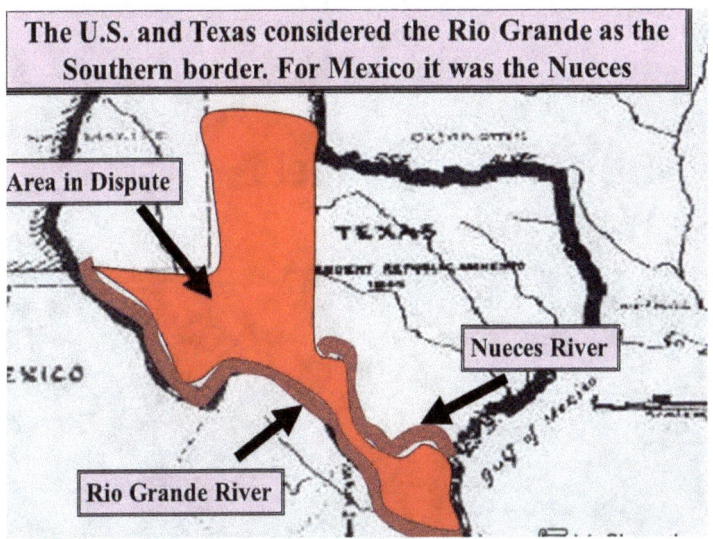

My great-grandparents were living in the bottom of the red area in 1848 before the border moved from the Nueces River to the Rio Grande River.

Section E is the area where my great-grandparents lived prior to the border move in 1848.

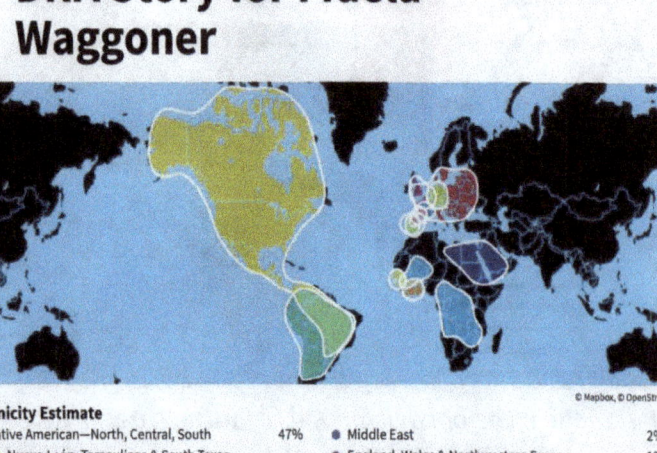

A few years ago, I did my Ancestry DNA test to be sure that I was telling my story correctly.

My freshman year was also the year that President Kennedy was assassinated. It was during our lunch period so we were unaware of what had just happened. I had English class after lunch, with the teacher who was "surprised" that I did so well on my achievement tests. He was a large man, well over 300 pounds, and he was sitting at his desk, crying uncontrollably. We were all stunned and quietly settled into our desks. Seconds later, an announcement came over the intercom, "President Kennedy has been shot! He did not survive!" The whole class started crying. The boys were trying very hard not to cry but they did. What had just happened? Our president was gone. There was a war brooding in Vietnam. The world was changing. This added more fuel to my desire to find out what else was out there and how I could make a difference in the world. What was out there for me? Would I have enough courage to venture out to the unknown?

In my sophomore year, I attended Harlingen High School in the town where my oldest sister Esmeralda and her husband Martin lived. Although a foreign language was part of the curriculum, if you were Hispanic and were speaking Spanish on campus, you would be in trouble. It happened to me once and I argued strongly that I was simply studying my lesson. It was not a convincing statement, so I had to stay in the detention hall. This was another example of how indigenous people speaking their native tongue were treated differently. I lived with Esmeralda and Martin that year and helped care for my niece when she was born that summer.

My junior and senior years were spent back at Lyford High School. I loved sports and wanted to play basketball and run track, but our father did not approve of women wearing shorts. Plus, he was so busy that he could not take me or pick me up from practice if I had stayed after school. I did participate in different clubs and got rides from friends if necessary. In my senior year, I was part of the senior play. I wanted to play a role but did not get one. However, I was the stage manager and coordinated the actors, made sure the costumes were clean and ready, that everyone knew their lines, and so forth. Then I would sit in the audience with our director (the extra big English teacher). I guess maybe even back then, my leadership skills were identified, although I would rather have had a part in the play. Life happens...

Chapter Four
Graduation, Now What?

Two weeks after graduation, I was supposed to start picking cotton as I had done almost every summer since I could pull a 100-pound sack of cotton. My innate desire for something more than what I had was always front and center. I knew that staying there on the farm or in Lyford meant no future at all. But then again, what had I planned for my life? Maybe "no future at all" was a little harsh thinking, but I knew that staying in South Texas just was not an option. My mother understood that more than anyone else. She was the most caring and understanding person I knew, and very wise. She realized what I had to do and would later help my father understand that too. That feeling in my gut that there was more to life persisted, but, being raised in a very sheltered environment with strict morals and values, it was going to be difficult to break out. But difficulty never stopped me. I was quickly realizing that life itself is not easy, so I had to make the best of it.

Summer of 1967, I spent with my oldest sister and helped with babysitting. This was an alternative to picking cotton and Esmeralda needed help with her daughter. My thoughts always came back to, "How do I leave the security of my home to venture into the unknown safely?" I realized that I had grandiose ideas but maybe not the courage to act. On one of my sister's weekdays off work, I walked to the downtown Air Force recruiting office and enlisted for four years. There were only two things standing in the way. One of them, I could work on and overcome. The other called for reinforcements and a strategic plan in order to win.

Number one was that I was overweight. The charts back then showed that if I was 5 feet 5 inches tall, my weight had to be no more than 125 pounds; I was 135. I just wouldn't eat tortillas for a while and would lose the extra weight. The second was more difficult. My father had to give permission. Boys were being drafted right out of high school, but girls had to get permission from their parents if they were under 21. Needless to say, my father would not sign. My mother could not sign because she was unable to write at that time. My father's feeling was typical of a man's thoughts back then: women go into the service to serve the men. I was upset that he would think that of me. They had raised me better than that. Why would I mess up my life like that? However, he objected. I finally gave him my ultimatum: "You will sign the form or I will hitchhike to California by myself." Up against the wall, he signed. I am not really sure whether I would have hitchhiked, but it sure scared him enough to sign. He probably wondered where I came from. In our Hispanic culture, the man is the patriarch and no child questions or goes against the father's wishes. Maybe it was the early beginnings of "women's lib." I knew that life had more to offer and although I was scared to death to leave the safety of my home, I wanted to do it. My sights were set for California, however I could get there. It was the sixties and life was happening outside of the Rio Grande Valley. I felt like this could be the beginning of the rest of my life.

I had made my decision. As soon as I met all criteria, I would be on my way to my future. My fears, as well as those of my parents, about leaving the safety of my home were eliminated. I would be under the safety of the United States Air Force. How more safe and secure could I be? I supposed my father may have realized that and may have even been a little proud of me. I was going to serve my country, not the servicemen. I am not sure whether my father ever understood me or why I was so different from the others. I know he worried about me and he never told me how he felt. He was a man of few words. The best part of coming home on leave was not that I would see all my siblings and Mom, but rather the trip to the airport with my father at the end of my visit. That was when we had an opportunity to say something to each other but didn't. We drove in silence, knowing that when we stopped and he walked me into the small airport, I would receive the biggest hug as I whispered in his ear, "Love you, dad." He never said it back but the tight sweet hug that followed was enough to know he loved me. There are times now when I really need a hug from my dad. It was because he loved me that he had to finally let me go. My

California dreaming was never going to go away. I was excited to experience life outside the Valley and yet apprehensive about the world out there. However, I knew that I could always come home. The question was, would I want to?

I spent most of the fall of 1967 eating rice cakes and water. No tortillas for me or anything that would put any pounds on my body. When the recruiter called and said there was a spot for me, I was excited yet nervous. I had never been outside of the small community we lived in. I had never been in an airplane so I chose to ride the bus to San Antonio. However, living with a bunch of women was going to be no different than living with my seven sisters at home. Discipline? No problem. We had rules and chores at home. I was always ready for a challenge. Let the adventure begin. I was going to make as much out of life as I could with the limited knowledge I had. But remember, I learn very well. I was so ready.

February 1968: Basic training graduation picture.

Life Happens, Keep Moving Forward

Chapter Five
Serving My Country

Scared yet excited, in January 1968 I boarded a bus that took me out of the Valley to San Antonio, Texas, and a whole new life. This was the first time I had left home and gone so far away. My stomach was so full of butterflies I thought I would just float away from all of their activity. I still felt apprehension about leaving the safety of home for the unknown, but I ventured forward. No turning back now. Life happens...

Basic training was difficult, but I was used to carrying 100 pounds of cotton, so all the physical conditioning did not bother me. What I had an issue with was all the available food. I had never had three square meals a day with dessert. Going through the "chow line" was like being a kid in a candy factory. I wanted one of everything. Unfortunately, the more you eat, the bigger you get. I almost did not get out of basic training due to my weight. I had gained back most of the ten pounds I had lost in order to join. I also started a bad habit then. My roommate introduced me to cigarettes. Glad to say, that only lasted a year or two.

The six weeks of basic training went by quickly and I was assigned to a base in North Texas for training as a medical service technician, or medic. I was happy with that since my favorite subjects and best grades were in the sciences. My quest to get to California was still at the forefront of my mind. As we got closer to graduation from medic school, we were allowed to request bases where we wanted to be stationed. My first choice was Travis AFB in northern California because, on the map, it looked like it was only an inch from San Francisco. My goal was to go to Haight Ashbury and see the "hippies." I felt like I was a "flower child" trying to bust out of my traditional quiet introverted self. Getting stationed at your first-choice base depended on your grades. That was no issue for me. It was science and I was learning so much. We had an exercise in which we rescued patients from a crashed airplane in the dark, while it was snowing. It was a great experience but at the time, I thought I would never survive it, much less my patient. After a short visit with family, I was on my way to California in an airplane, another first for me. Let the adventures begin! Life happens....

On leave and hanging out with my brothers Rick, Fidel, Benny, and Jimmy. Louie is the baby and Abel is likely outdoors.

On leave after medic training visiting my parents before leaving for California.

We lived within an hour's drive of South Padre Island. My siblings always enjoyed going to the beach when I came home on leave. Five brothers and three sisters younger than me. Left to right, back row: Fidel (11), Abel (14), Jimmy (16), Della (21), Marina (13), and Albino Jr/Benny (7). Front row: Eva (9), Dora (5), and Louie (3).

My job at Travis AFB was to care for the dependent children of service families. I thought the pediatric unit was a great place to work, but unfortunately, the children were sick and, in some cases, terminally ill. I did not know it at the time, but I was about to meet a child with a condition that would show up later in my life. That condition would change the direction of our lives and create a bond in our family that would help with our salvation.

I saw a captain and his wife standing by their child's crib, both of them crying. I was nineteen at the time and not long at this duty assignment. I asked the Lieutenant why they were crying and what was wrong with the little girl. The words she said would be repeated to me by a neurologist 17 years later in reference to our own baby. "She has a disease called Werdnig-Hoffmann Syndrome, so she will not survive." I did not understand. She was beautiful with big brown eyes and long eyelashes. Those parents had obviously received the same prognosis as we would years later. "Your child will drown in his or her own secretions. There is nothing that can be done. Treatment is supportive care." Soon, more terminally ill kids came in, so I started looking for another department because I was getting too attached to my patients. Life happens...

The final straw came when I was assisting a young girl with a condition known as osteogenesis imperfecta or brittle bone disease. She was a delightful, bright, intelligent 11-year-old lying in a special Circ-o-electric bed so she could be moved without breaking her bones. I did not understand then what that disease did to the inside of her body. I could only see the damage from the outside. My last day in the pediatric unit was the day I was helping with her care and she "coded" while I was talking to her. At first, I was not sure what was happening. I kept calling her name but she did not respond so I ran out of the room and down the hall yelling to the nurses that something was wrong. The Code Team came in and tried to resuscitate her while I waited in the utility room, crying. When they were done, I had to go in and clean her up. I think I cried the whole time and was glad no one had offered to help me. She had brittle bones so doing CPR only crushed her chest. It is difficult to get that image out of my head. I will always remember Donna. Life happens... and sometimes, it sucks!

One of the best things that happened while stationed at Travis was the friends I made. I was part of a group of four guys (Manny, Tommy, Jim, and Will) and four girls (Mary, Julie, Debbie, and me) who all went to parties together. Most of the time, I was the designated person that made sure everyone got home safely. It was a wonderful relationship until, as was inevitable, some of the participants started liking each other and not only that, one pair got married! That messed up the whole platonic relationship thing. Those two friends are still married. We were all 19- and 20-year-olds trying to navigate life while serving our country. Friendships made for life. We enjoyed this relationship until we started getting orders for other places in the world. Two of the girls and one guy stayed at Travis their entire tour. Two of us went to the Philippines, one to Tully, Greenland, one to Japan, and one to Vietnam. I have been able to reconnect with five of the seven friends.

Life Happens, Keep Moving Forward

Jim Coella (Debbie's boyfriend). Mary, me, and Manny at the San Franciso Zoo.

Left to right, back row: Della, Julie, and Mary. Front: Will, Tommy, and unknown. Will and Julie would later marry.

Della and Mary

Mary, Tommy, and me in front. Debbie and Manny in back. First Christmas together.

Life Happens, Keep Moving Forward

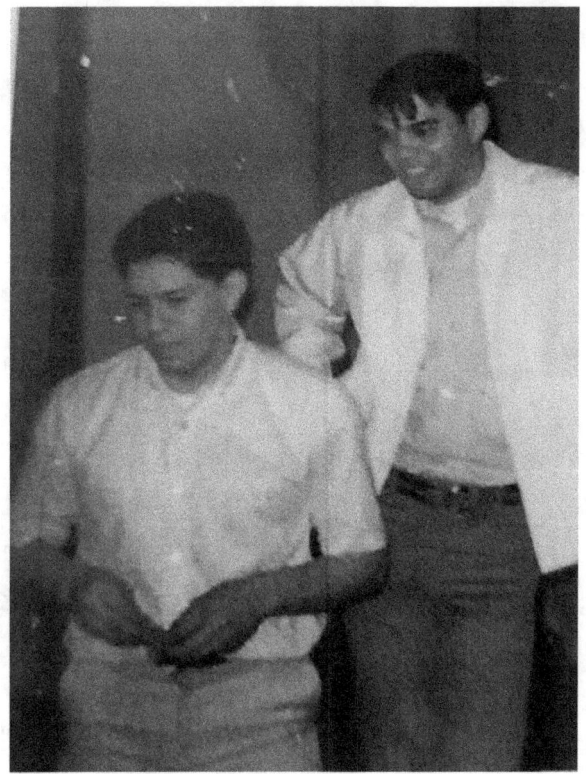

Manny and Tommy.

I had another friend who worked in the dental office. He was the only other Hispanic person at the base hospital. It was the sixties and we were in California, just a one-hour drive from San Francisco, and we went to as many concerts as we could. He invited me to a concert in Berkeley one summer Saturday. It was great, the music was outstanding. It was at the park at the University of California. Sitting on the lawn, watching hippies smoke grass and listening to wonderful music from Joan Baez, Steve Miller... At that moment, life was great. This is why I wanted to come to California. It was great until my friend accepted an offer to go on stage to speak against the war. Finally, the little sheltered girl from South Texas got it! It was an anti-war demonstration and my Air Force buddy, Dave, was on stage saying something about "the Mickey Mouse organization at Travis." About that time, someone handed me a "joint." Not knowing what to do with it, I handed it to the person next to me. Apparently, that was proper etiquette for smoking pot. We returned to base that evening and he dropped me off at my barracks. Shortly after arriving at work on Monday, I was called to the phone by my charge nurse, the Major. The person on the other end did not sound very nice. He wanted to know if I had been at Peace Park in Berkeley that Saturday. In my meek little voice, I answered, "Yes." He then informed me that I was to come down to the Air Police station immediately. My lame excuse of "I have my patients to care for" did not matter, so I took a cab to the front entrance of the base where the Air Police station was located. Another learning experience followed as I navigated myself through life with very little "street know-how." It reminded me of Arlo Guthrie's 1967 Alice's Restaurant.

I was fingerprinted, had a mugshot, and everything else there at the police station. "And what were you arrested for?" Not for littering! In my case, I was arrested for being a pinko, nazi commie! Or at least, that was my feeling. According to my friends, back at the hospital, I was gone all day. As I remember, I was on the hot seat so I did seem to be there all day. I think what finally ended the "interrogation" was when the Tech Sergeant asked me if I slept with my friend who was with me. I was incensed that he had the nerve to ask me that since it had nothing to do with the issue. I very sternly said to him, "What does that have to do with it and he is like a brother, so NO!" He then excused me and I returned to work. My shift was over by that time. Dave and I never discussed it other than he had also been called in. I figured he got into more trouble since he voiced his opinion about the Air Force while we were there. Later, we realized that undercover air police were likely in attendance. I was so glad I had not smoked that joint someone passed me. Almost fifty years later, I would find my "radical" friend and I lived just a few miles from each other. It was great to reminisce and meet his beautiful wife and son. Unfortunately, just a few months after meeting his wife, she passed away. We stay in touch, and meet at a blues club occasionally, enjoying each other's company as when we were 20 years old.

Relationships with men were difficult for me. I always felt like my father was watching over me, reminding me that my purpose in the service was not for the men. My first experience with "love" or what I thought was love was actually domestic abuse. He was handsome with beautiful blue eyes, and I fell hard. However, it did not take long to realize that he was using me. It was the day I was at his place and he received a call from a woman telling him that her 17-year-old daughter had just given birth to his son. I was stunned. As he left to see his new son, his roommate said to me, "Della, you don't deserve this. You deserve better. I can take you back to the barracks." While I was heartbroken, I was glad to see that not all men were self-centered. After a good cry, I did what I knew how to do best. I would move on and be glad I was not that 17-year-old girl, although my heart went out to her. She had been deceived more than I had. I was rid of him and knew I would be okay. When I thought about it, I realized that he only came to get me from the base for his own pleasure. We never went to a movie or on a date. In fact, I don't even remember if he ever kissed me or told me he even cared about me. Obviously, his only interest in me was below the waist. I guess I thought that was okay until it was not.

About a week after the baby episode, he came to "pick me up." The barracks always had a person on duty at the front office area, and she knew not to get me or let him in. I refused to come down. I could see him from my window. I knew he would be angry when he got back to his truck, but I was finally done with him. Little did I know that men like him do not like to lose. So, the stalking began. Eventually, he got the number for our phone in our barracks room. How did that happen? There was an "open house" celebration in our barracks where families of the airmen and women could come to visit. The barracks were open to the public so families could see how and where their loved ones lived and served. Imagine my surprise when I entered my room and found him standing there trying to pick up my roommate! She either gave him the number or he saw it on the phone; either way, he had our phone number. He proceeded to call constantly soon after. I worked the night shift at that time and it was difficult to sleep with the phone ringing at all hours day or night. I didn't know that you could unplug the phone to stop the calls. Soon after that, my roommate received orders and since the phone was hers, she disconnected it. That likely saved my sanity, and I was able to get rid of the stalker.

I was always afraid that he would find me. It was a huge base, but I found myself looking over my shoulder whenever I was out. This was my first experience with a man, and it turned out to be what my father had said. He just wanted sex and had absolutely no respect for me. Later I realized that this was not love but a selfish, evil person who only loved himself and if I had stayed in that relationship, I would not have survived. Domestic violence is real and, unfortunately, many times a life is lost. Of course, I went on to have other relationships, but I learned to be very careful and particular about who I trusted and who I let into my heart. Remember that I learn quickly. I am happy to say that most of the young men I dated were kind and gentlemen. Most of them may have wanted more but I had learned from my experience. Respecting oneself can be difficult when you make a mistake even though you know better. Life happens...

By this time, I had achieved some rank and was able to live off base. My friend Julie, whose husband had been sent to a base in Greenland, my roommate Karen, from the barracks, and I moved into an apartment. Later we rented a house shortly after one of my sisters came out from Texas.

In the fall of 1969, my younger sister, Virginia, came to California after her graduation. I enjoyed my life off base and having my sister around kept me from getting homesick. I bought my first car, a 1966 Plymouth Valiant, and I had a dog named Ackley. I worked in a urology clinic with three urologists and three male technicians. It was interesting work with an interesting group. The doctors were nice although there was one who still had very deep roots in the Civil War South. It was not unusual to hear him refer to our Black patients by the N word, although he did not say it to their faces. It upset me, but he was a Major and I was a Sergeant, so I kept my mouth shut.

The technicians were mostly nice, although there is always that one creep in every office. It is interesting to me that some men would think of women as just objects to be played with, emotionally and physically. I realize now that there were incidents throughout my tour that qualified as harassment, but it was never discussed. I remember going to the Central Supply department for supplies and when I entered, the airmen there all snickered and left the front area. I picked up my supplies and asked why everyone was laughing. Had I missed the joke? The response was so embarrassing that I left without my supplies. "We have a pool going on how big your boobs are." I was 22 and somewhat naive. Nowadays, I would have responded, "40D, who won?" It still would have upset me but at least they would not have known it. When the MeToo movement took off, I was delighted. But it is disheartening to know that some men have gotten into very high positions in this country even though they abused women all their lives. Some of them even become President. Life happens…

I was settling into my role as a sergeant, working in a clinic, weekends and holidays off when Uncle Sam snapped me into reality. You've got mail! My orders were to leave after a two-week visit with family. I was to report to Clark AFB Philippines January 1971. The usual assignment was an 18-month tour of duty, however, since I only had 11 months left in my 4-year commitment, I was allowed to serve just the 11months. I packed all my belongings into my car, and my sister, my dog and I made the four-day drive back to Texas. I gave my car and my dog to my dad, said goodbye to the family and set my sights for the Philippines. I was excited about going to the Philippines. I thought that it was a country whose main language was Spanish and I would be able to interact with the locals without any problem. Unfortunately, I had forgotten my history lessons. The Northern part of the Philippines was not settled by Spaniards as I thought; therefore, they spoke a different dialect, Tagalog. Although some of the words are derived from Spanish, it's not the same. I was able to understand some of it and was proud of that. Later, I would find out a little more about the language and indigenous people living on the base.

A Negrito village within the base. These indigenous people were allowed to stay in their meager dwellings within the base.

Chapter Six
Reality Check

It was cold in January in Northern California as I donned my dress blues and boarded the plane for the 15-hour flight to Clark Air Base. I was excited and full of anticipation. I was going to a country that spoke my language (I thought) and it was only an 11-month tour, so I would be out by the end of the year. We stopped in Hawaii to refuel but it was late at night, and I could not see anything other than the flight line. Continuing on, we landed in the Philippines the next morning. As I stepped off the plane, the atmosphere immediately hit me. My dress blues stuck to me as the amount of perspiration escaping every pore in my body felt like glue. The air was so thick with humidity it was difficult to breathe. Had the airplane taken a wrong turn? Had we landed back home in South Texas? The moisture in the air was incredible. It reminded me of home and the feeling of clothes sticking to your body on hot summer days. Someone was there to meet me and take me to my new barracks. She greeted me and began our acquaintance by telling me about "someone getting murdered for $5.00 because she was messing with an airman who was married to a local lady." She also informed me that the local language is Tagalog, the Indonesian language of the Malayan people of the Philippines, not Spanish. I was not sure how I was going to like this place and my excitement started to fade.

We arrived at the barracks and I quickly changed out of my drippy dress blues into some shorts. The barracks were not air conditioned and bugs and geckos became our guests. It reminded me of life at the farm with the cockroaches who greeted me every morning and scattered when the light came on. Some of the homes outside the base were made of cardboard and the poverty of that country was so real. The town right outside the base was not a good example of the people and their culture. Its streets were lined with bars and women ready to make a quick buck. The music was familiar as I heard a local band attempting to sing Pretty Woman by Roy Orbison. Somehow it didn't sound very pretty. And then there was the monsoon season six months out of the year when it rained continuously.

*Jeepneys, the main mode of transportation.
Be sure to keep arms inside the vehicle at all times.*

The main method of transportation was a jeepney. Decorated with colors and streamers, it's a type of jeep like a bus that goes faster than it should. It can also climb up the sidewalk and careen off walls as it makes its way through the streets. People can fall out or lose a limb from "not keeping all arms and legs inside." There was also a bus known as The Rabbit that was used for traveling between provinces. Often pigs, chickens and rabbits were among the passengers. All trips included pit stops along the way so the men could get out and relieve themselves against the wheels of the bus. The women had to wait. I was a nurse in training at the time so waiting was good practice for me. My days off were spent visiting the country outside of the base with friends. The base was in the Northern part of the Philippines, close to Manila, the capital city. My first visit to Manila landed me in the hospital with food poisoning.

My friend and fellow medic and I saw diplomats having lunch in the restaurant next to the American Embassy, so we thought it would be a safe place to eat. Unfortunately, we were wrong. Everything was delicious until 12 hours later when it all came up with a vengeance. I was in the hospital for two days due to severe dehydration. After that, we decided that the chow hall on base was the safest place to eat. I found out later that it likely was the ice in my drink that made me sick. Giardia runs rampant in the water, hiding in plain sight in the ice cubes. Life happens…

Clark AFB, Philippines.

Clark AFB Hospital

I was assigned to the orthopedic unit at the base hospital. I didn't think that would be too bad. Broken bones, etc. Was I in for a surprise. Most of the "boys" or soldiers on that unit had been injured in Vietnam. Some of them had legs and arms missing. All of a sudden, the war was real. The Buffalo Springfield band was singing in my ear.

> "There's something happening here.
>
> What it is not exactly clear.
>
> There's a man with a gun over there
>
> Telling me I got to beware.
>
> There are battle lines being drawn
>
> Nobody's right if everybody's wrong
>
> Young people speaking their minds
>
> Getting so much resistance from behind."

No more sick babies or checking urinary systems as I had done at the clinic at Travis AFB. This was reality. These young men were my age or younger. They had dreams of going to college, raising a family, and growing old together with their loved ones. I took care of a 19-year-old with a track scholarship, a 4-year full ride, who now found himself with no legs; they were amputated above the knees. How does one deal with that? He cried a lot and I tried to comfort him but "everything was not going to be alright."

When you go back home, the citizens that you fought for, the ones you lost your legs for, will call you names and shun you, and pretend that you do not exist. They will also call you "baby killers." The sight of you in your wheelchair with no legs and a tin can in your hands, asking for "spare change" will make them turn away and feel pity. They do not realize that it is they who should be pitied. They missed an opportunity to meet a real hero. A hero is measured by the lives he saved and sacrifices he made, not by the number of touchdowns, baskets or home runs he achieved. I always wondered what happened to those young men. Did they make it home? Are they still alive? Do they know that I still think of them? Did I pass one on the street and not know it? Sometimes, I find myself staring or looking at a man with no legs around my age and wanting to ask him who he is and how he lost his legs. Did I care for him at one time?

There was different equipment to learn to operate, like the Stryker frame, Thomas leg splints, Steinmann pins, and on-the-job training for open wounds. Some of the injuries were pretty horrific but even though my first thought was, "This is not what I signed up for," yet it was. Here is where I could make a difference. This tour of duty would end up being the most rewarding and educational of my time served. One young man was in a circle bed because nearly all his bones had been broken when he fell from a helicopter. He had been injured and was being airlifted by cable up to a helicopter but halfway up, the cable broke and he fell more than 100 feet to the ground. He was suffering from pressure ulcers, one of the problems with being in one position for a long period. Three of his four extremities were in some type of traction, so his movement was very limited. One day when I arrived at work, he was yelling and screaming at the top of his lungs. I thought maybe his traction had broken. We quickly realized he was covered with "sugar ants" and was being bitten all over. Apparently one of the treatments for pressure ulcers back then had a substantial amount of sugar in it (nowadays, we use Medi honey). The entire staff worked together to stabilize his traction so we could get to his bottom and get the ants out. It was difficult but I was glad that his traction was intact. Months later, his wounds were healed enough that he could be put in a body cast and shipped closer to home in the States. We had to wait until the body cast dried completely, then we proceeded to "bivalve" the entire cast. Since he was being transported to the US in a military non pressurized aircraft, it was essential that the cast allowed for expansion. The patient's body would become edematous (puffy) and a cast that wouldn't expand would be detrimental to the patient. I learned how to operate a hand saw as I worked diligently to cut the cast all the way around the body. We then had to ace wrap the entire cast so that it would stabilize the patient's fractured bones yet would "give" as his body swelled in a non-pressurized airplane.

There was the 19-year-old who purposely tried to shoot his big toe off so he would not have to go back to the war. Unfortunately, we fixed it and sent him back. I always wondered if Hutchinson made it home alive. Then there was Carl, who had lost his left foot. He joked and laughed but sometimes it was hard to hide his pain. Life happens…

I had a great mentor during this part of my service. He and I were responsible for changing all the bandages on patients' wounds. My instructions outside the room of the first patient went like this: "These wounds are pretty graphic. You must be sure not to show any type of disgust. These young men will see that as a form of rejection. They see you as their girlfriend, sister, or mother and your response to their situation is critical. I will be there with you and we will do this together." He was not kidding! My first patient was a Native American from Arizona who had lost most of the calf on his left leg, which I could see from the doorway although it was bandaged. His right leg had been traumatically amputated by a landmine above the knee. It also was bandaged. My mentor started by introducing me to our patient and telling him that I was in training and was going to assist with his dressing change. The patient agreed. I moved into position to hold up his thigh so my mentor could remove the old dressing. As we got closer to the wound, he asked me to change positions with him so I could finish removing the bandage. I moved, but instead of moving to the patient's side to hold the thigh for me, he stood right behind me. I was perplexed and wondered why he was standing so close that I could almost feel his breath on the back of my neck. I continued removing the dressings and talking to our patient. As I removed that last layer of gauze, the bone and flesh were exposed. It looked like ham from the farm. All I could think was "do not show any disgust" and then my knees went weak. As I started to head down, I felt a knee at the back of my left thigh. I nonchalantly leaned against his knee, shifted my weight and continued changing the dressing. My mentor did not have to pick me up off the floor and my patient never knew what happened. I was lucky to have such an insightful person to show me the way. I would develop very strong feelings for this young man but alas, he had a girlfriend at home that he would eventually marry. He was a great teacher and, obviously, an honorable man as he stayed true to his girlfriend.

I became very skilled at wrapping a "residual limb" so that the dressing does not slip off. The remainder of an amputated leg or arm is not called a "stump" but rather, a residual limb. That would be significant later in my career as a rehab nurse. The year spent at Clark AFB was the most rewarding part of my tour and also the saddest, due to the stark reality of war and its destruction of lives, hopes, and dreams. I learned a lot that year about myself. I realized that traumatic wounds did not frighten me and if I could help those young soldiers, then maybe I could help others in the future. My decision was made. At some point, I would go to school and become a nurse.

Every Sunday afternoon, we received a flight of horribly injured South Korean soldiers who were helping us with the fight in Vietnam. An American service family whose husband was stationed there "adopted" one of our Korean patients. Although US citizens would show no appreciation for returning soldiers, that mindset was even worse in South Korea. The United States usually provided education and medical care for the wounded, but a South Korean soldier who came home without limbs was a disgrace to his country. Some took their own lives because of this cultural belief. That family explained all this to me. I was saddened to think that this young man may not live out his life as he was supposed to.

The favorite meal of Koreans is a cabbage soup called Kimchi. It's what beans and tortillas are to my culture. I remember very distinctly the first Sunday afternoon I worked there. The "chow wagon" came down the hall and we descended on it to get trays to distribute to our patients. It must have been a rite of passage to let the new guy open up the cart. Oh my God! The aroma that rose from that cart as the door flew open was enough to knock you over. It smelled like something very rotten had died a long time ago. But the smiles on the faces of those Korean soldiers, when they got their meal, were well worth the traumatic attack on my olfactory nerves. These guys hated the Viet Cong, and the story was that when they killed them, they mutilated their bodies. I was glad they were on our side. As my tour of duty was coming to an end, I again began to wonder what was next in my life. Life happens...

On my days off, I often traveled to Baguio, a province up in the mountains. It was cool up there and you could enjoy the beautiful country without getting too uncomfortable. My friends and I would go into town during the day to shop for material and meet with one of many seamstresses who would make whatever you desired. They reminded me of my sister, Mary, who made sewing look so easy. The nightlife was not too exciting for ladies as most of the entertainment was for men. I had an opportunity to go on leave during my tour, so my friend Donna and I decided to go to Hong Kong. As servicewomen, we could hop a ride on aircraft leaving Clark AFB and go wherever they were heading.

We signed out and went to the airport ready to go on vacation to a tropical country. Unfortunately, we did not check well enough, and it turned out there was no plane going to Hong Kong, but there was one going to Japan. Since we were already signed out on leave, we took that flight. When we arrived at Yokota AFB in Japan it was snowing! We were picked up by other ladies in the Air Force, who wondered why we were dressed inappropriately, so our first stop was at the BX (base exchange) to purchase winter clothes. This was the first time I had seen a car with the steering wheel on the passenger side. My friend Donna took all the pictures and unfortunately, I never asked her for copies. The other sad thing is that I cannot remember her last name. All I recall is that she was from Rhode Island and was a blonde Scandinavian lady who was over 6 feet tall. It was quite interesting the looks we got from the Japanese men on the subway. They just stared at her!

My tour was almost over, and I was ready to go home. I wonder sometimes why I was so eager to go home when I did not have a plan. I said goodbye to friends I had made there at Clark AFB and as Christmas 1971 was approaching, I began to think about returning to Texas.

I had just spent a year caring for our soldiers. I had seen and learned so much and yet I was still feeling uneasy about venturing back into civilian life. I learned that one of my sister's classmates had been killed in Vietnam. He was the first one in our hometown. I could not imagine how those parents felt after losing a son. Unfortunately, I would know that in the future. Later I would visit the Vietnam Memorial where I looked for his name on the wall. Visiting the memorial is emotionally overwhelming. Although I did not know him personally, I knew his family when I was growing up. When I found his name, I took a picture of it and etched his name on the paper provided by the guard. I made sure his family in my hometown received it.

Martin Cavazos' name on the Vietnam War Memorial in Washington, DC.

Lance Corporal Martin Cavazos, US Marine Corps. Permission from Daniel Cavazos, brother of Martin.

Chapter Seven
Return to Civilian Life

I am not really sure why I did not just stay in the Air Force. The war was still on and our commander in chief was in big trouble, something about Watergate. The sixties were over, but our country was still in turmoil. The war would come to an end later that year, but the pain would continue. It was a terrible war that took so many of our brothers and sisters. There were no winners, least of all, the American and Vietnamese people. Why? Politics? Of course, that seems to be the root of all evil. Unfortunately, that continues to be true today.

My sister, Virginia, had talked about returning to California with me once I was discharged but there was no solid plan there. When I returned, I found that she was starting a family and staying in Houston. This just meant that I would go to Plan B; however, I did not have one. Life happens…

My life was evolving but I did not know what it was evolving to. I moved in with my sister and her husband in a rented house in Houston. Why did it always seem like I was chasing an elusive dream? What was that dream? I knew I liked helping people, so I thought I should look for something that would make me feel good at the end of the day. Unfortunately, having lots of experience but no degree got me nowhere.

The thought of using my GI benefits to attend school had not even entered my mind at that point. It had been 4 years since I left high school and yet I seemed to be at the same crossroads. What was I afraid of?

Living in Houston after discharge from the Air Force. Flower child returned to Texas.

I had been a Medical Service Technician in the United States Air Force, so I was ready to work at my profession and save the world! That bubble burst very quickly when I applied for work. Although I had gained tremendous experience as a medic, I did not have a degree, certificate or anything that would get me a better job other than as a nurse's aide in a nursing home. Don't get me wrong, caring for the elderly is an honorable job but in 1972, the minimum wage was $1.65 an hour for a nursing assistant. However, because I had so much experience, I started at $1.80 per hour. I took the job and stayed for three weeks. Somehow, the other nursing assistants found out I was getting paid more than they were although they had been there a while. I had just gotten back from patching up broken soldiers and I was not in the mood for a bunch of whining women, especially for 15 cents more pay. I quit that job and started working in an electronics factory on an assembly line. That was worse than the previous job although it paid better and had benefits. I tried very hard to acclimate to life in Texas again, but that monotonous job on that assembly line was not very exciting. For some reason, I was not pursuing college yet. Was it that lack of confidence so prominent in high school that still lingered? Or was it that no one was there to tell me that I could do it? I am not really sure why I felt that way, but I knew that I was not happy in my situation, so as always, California came calling.

In January 1973, I hitched a ride with a cousin and her family who were driving back to California. We drove for 2 days straight, with no stops except to go to the bathroom. I stayed with them for a few days, then took a bus to Vacaville, outside of Travis AFB, where an old Air Force roommate was living. Again, the question came to mind, "Is this all there is?" The answer was a resounding NO! I got a job down the street at a hamburger joint that was becoming very popular at the time. It had golden arches and a clown as its chief operating officer. As soon as I saved enough money, I bought a little Fiat and answered an ad for "live-in caregiver needed." It was a delightful couple who were almost too generous for what little I did for them. I think they just wanted a "granddaughter" around the house. That voice in my head kept bugging me. Why did I not just enroll in college and use my benefits? I would have an income and learn something. Something kept holding me back. I was afraid! I did not think I could make it in college. I think that I thought I was not smart enough for college even though I considered myself a "woman of the world" due to my life experiences. Was the thought of failing too scary? To prove myself wrong, I enrolled in the local community college full-time. Health and science interested me, so that was a start, especially if my eventual goal was nursing.

I left that sweet couple after I was hired at a hospital and learned a new job, sterilizing surgical instruments. The job was very interesting and since I had never been in a surgical setting, I enjoyed learning the names of all the instruments and what they were used for. This was when I met a beautiful couple who would take me under their wing and nurture me.

Ruby and Dave would become my surrogate parents and ensure I was always safe. We would lose Ruby in 2003. I found out the day I was recovering from breast cancer surgery. A few years later, their daughter Monica would be gone. She was so young, and I never really found out what happened. Just a few months ago, we lost Dave. He had lived a long life and missed his wife and daughter. We have Mike left from that family. We continue to see each other as he is still considered a surrogate brother.

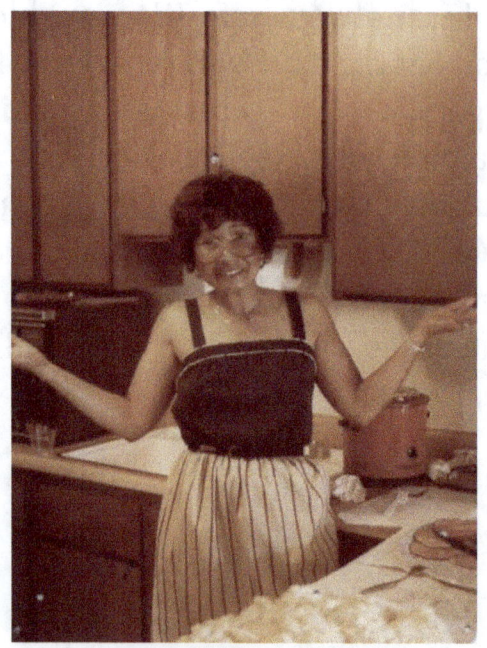
Ruby Davenport

Monica & Jerome "Dave" Davenport

During this time, I was introduced to people with alternative lifestyles. Although I was aware that there were people who liked people of the same gender, I had not been exposed to that lifestyle yet. In the Air Force I had a roommate who was gay but she never discussed it with me. Years later, I ran into her at this same hospital and she commented on that, saying "I knew you were straight, so I never thought about approaching you."

I met a young man, Fred, at work who was divorced. Before I could assume any possibility of a relationship, I found out that women were not his choice of partners. However, we became best friends and have been to this day. I later learned that several members of my family had alternative lifestyles. God creates all kinds of folks. I think it's his way of challenging us to be better humans. Unfortunately, there are several who cannot or will not accept that challenge. He keeps trying! Life happens...

Fred and me, 50 years later. Still great friends.

I was enjoying my new life, going to school, working, and making new friends. However, I continued to feel a responsibility to help at home, whether with finances or just being there when needed. In the spring 1974, I was notified that my mother was having some health issues. The toll of multiple births with little time between for her body to recover plus other general medical issues caused my mother's health to deteriorate quickly. She had been hospitalized several times without a definite diagnosis, so she was transported to the big medical center in Galveston, Texas. She was unable to speak English well enough to make her needs known and fearful of not knowing what was wrong. I felt terrible that my beautiful mother, who was always there for us and gave her all, was now alone. Houston was only an hour away and my oldest sister lived there, so I went to be with her. On August 4, 1974, while I was sitting at her bedside, my momma, Josefa Perez Olivarez, left for heaven. At the time, I was not a nurse, so I had no real understanding of what had just happened. She was still young with much to live for. She had finally gotten her brick house with indoor plumbing. Her youngest child was only in second grade.

From left to right, me, Ema, Virginia, Marina (the baby), my beautiful mother Josefa, and one of my younger brothers, Abel.

She was only 50 but had lived a lifetime. Her struggles were over. It turned out that she had had heart disease and needed bypass surgery to get blood flow to her heart. We were all devastated. Her youngest child was 7 and there were still 6 kids in school. My father was lost without her and now had six children to continue raising without his wife. I stayed with the family for a year after she died and attempted to help. That was quite difficult, having been away from home and having changed so much. My 16-year-old sister, who had been helping our father while Mom was in the hospital, was basically running things. She knew the household, the kids' needs, and dad's medication. In order to provide some income for the family, I enrolled in a licensed vocational nursing program at a local hospital. It was the same one my older sister had graduated from. I remember my father telling my mom when he did not want to sign for me to enlist, "Why doesn't she just go to the same program her sister went to?" The defiant 18-year-old then responded with, "I don't want to be a nurse!" Now at 25, I was using my GI benefits to go to nursing school. I did want to be a nurse and I was looking for a BSN program; however, it turned out that being an LVN first helped tremendously. I worked for a short time in Texas after graduation, but that California bug was always hovering. My younger sister had proven herself to be a great chief operating officer and the family would be fine without me. They always had been. So, after a short three months working nights in the State hospital for mentally challenged adults, I made my decision to return to California. My father and the children were in good hands. Marina was in charge, and she knew how to take great care of the household. Momma would be as proud of her as I was.

Louie (7), me (25), Dorie (10), and Eva (14) at the farm after our mother died.

Left to right: Dora, Benny, Gloria (grandbaby), Louie, Fidel, and Eva. Dad is holding Jaime (grandbaby). Our old house that Dad built in the background.

Dad and I at the farm, 1975.

Mom had been gone for more than a year, so I said my goodbyes and Dad took me to the airport like he had so many times before. I got the big hug that I always looked forward to. I did not know that 6 months later he would also be gone. I always say he died of a broken heart. There is an actual condition called "broken heart syndrome" that occurs when couples who have been together for a long time lose their mate. I used to say that Dad couldn't find his socks without Mom. I guess he missed her too much. He also knew that the kids were going to be fine. He had seen my younger sister, the COO, in action. In July 1976, his heart was too broken to continue, and he joined his sweetheart in heaven.

Dad and me with his cows and Ackley, my dog that now belonged to him.

The year I spent at the farm after my mother died was extremely rewarding. I was able to go to nursing school and spend time with my younger siblings. I realized how little I knew about them. I had left when the youngest, Louie, was 14 months old, and now he was eight. He had just lost his mother and we did not know it then, but he was a juvenile diabetic. That would be discovered when he joined the Army after high school, when he would also discover that he was gay. I remember thinking that he was certainly "different" when I was there that year, but he was a young boy dealing with losing his mother. I had been in and out of his young life so much that he did not know me either. I am so happy that as adults we built a strong bond, because he is gone now too. He passed away at 52 but he had lived a lifetime and contributed so much. I am very proud of my youngest brother. I like to tell the story of when he "came out" to me.

The phone rang in the middle of the night, and I ran to the kitchen so as not to wake up my husband, Wayne. Who could be calling at this time of night? A late-night phone call brings a fear that someone in the family has been hurt or worse. It was Louie. The conversation went like this:

"I have something to tell you." I responded by saying, "Yes Louie, I know. You are gay and I love you. It's okay, go back to bed." His response, "But, but, but...how did you know?" "I knew when you were 8 and I lived with you guys after Mom died." How? "It does not matter, I love you, go to sleep."

Thus began a wonderful relationship with him and eventually with his wonderful husband, Stan. I will never understand why some people hate or don't accept people who are different. The saddest thing is that sometimes those folks proclaim to be "Christians." My response to them is, "God does not make mistakes."

My brother was not a mistake; he was a gift so that we could see life in a different light, because things are not always black and white. Sometimes they come as rainbows.

After many years together, Louie and Stan were able to marry. Unfortunately, we were unable to attend the wedding. It had been four months since we had lost Jeremy, and it was difficult for us to travel during our grieving process. Jeremy loved his uncles, and we knew that he would be there in spirit. Louie lived comfortably until leukemia took his life in 2020. He was 52. I am so glad I was able to spend time with him before he passed away.

Louie and I in Florida.

Louie was an amazing young man. He was able to run a marathon one year after his triple transplant surgery.

Louie and Stan on their wedding day.

Life Happens, Keep Moving Forward

Chapter Eight
Love and Challenges

I returned to California in 1975 as an LVN (Licensed Vocational Nurse). I applied for a position at the same hospital where I had learned to sterilize surgical instruments two years earlier.

My position was on an "as needed" basis, so I could continue to pursue my nursing career. I enrolled in a junior college "career mobility program" designed for those LVNs who wanted to enter the Associate Nursing Program (ANP). The ANP was an intensive one-year program for LVNs to become registered nurses. It did not include the leadership and management courses I would take later when earning my Bachelor's degree. Nonetheless, I was on my way to my ultimate goal.

There was a young man in my English class who looked very interesting to me with his long blonde hair, blue eyes, and beard. I saw him three days a week, standing outside the building our class was in, smoking a cigarette. He was friendly, attractive but too short. He was only about an inch taller than I was, and I was sure I had 15 or 20 pounds on him. So, we were cordial but nothing else. I received my first GI bill check, and then things changed. Life happens…

On April 1, 1976, I received my first check and showed it to that young man when I got to class. Turned out, he was also a veteran and was waiting for his first check. I needed to deposit my check of $1400, which was a lot of money at that time. He had a car, and I did not, so he offered to take me to the bank after class. I made the deposit and sent Dad some money for his birthday coming up on the 3rd. We ended up spending all evening together, talking for hours. He was amazing, interesting, cute, and kind. Who wouldn't like those attributes in a man? My general statement when people ask how we met is, "I took him home and he never left."

Three months later, I received that dreaded late evening phone call, "Your father has been taken to hospital." He was pronounced dead on arrival. I was stunned. How could that be? I knew he had heart issues, but he seemed fine 6 months ago when I left Texas. I think he just missed Mom too much and just could not survive without her. So, this kind young man accompanied me back to Texas to meet my father at his funeral. Every day I was falling in love with him more. Who would do this? He had only known me for three months. I found out later that my gay friends and my adopted Black family had all taken up a collection for him to accompany me to Texas and make sure I came back. While we were there, he met my brother-in-law, who offered him a job in the remodeling company he worked for in Houston. So, after we returned to

California, we finished up the semester and I turned in my notice at work. Then we packed up our bags, boarded our "hippie van" and headed to Texas. We really liked our van but after putting a new engine into it three different times, we finally traded it in for a family car after Ian was born.

Wayne and me on our way to Houston, Texas.

We moved to Houston so Wayne could work in construction, and I got a job as an LVN on a surgical unit at a hospital down the street from our apartment. I put my pursuit of an RN degree on hold for a while. We knew at this point that we were committed to each other and would likely get married once we were settled in and working. We would soon be challenged with the first big decision of our lives.

We did not have much money so it would have to be a small and inexpensive wedding. What we did not anticipate was that a month before the wedding, I would wake up with extreme nausea. I thought I had eaten something bad, remembering my episode in the Philippines. Unfortunately, it was not as simple as that. We had always been careful but all it took was only that one time. What to do was the question. We were not even talking about having children. We knew that we loved each other, but a child was not supposed to happen. After thinking about it, talking, and losing sleep, we decided that we could not have this child. It was the most difficult decision we had made up to that time. We could not know that life was only going to provide more difficult challenges in the future. Wayne's parents came from Arkansas for our very simple wedding in my oldest sister's backyard. His older brother was also getting married a week later, so they traveled on to Iowa for the next wedding.

Wayne and I, September 17, 1977 in Houston, Texas.

No one in either of our families ever knew except for one of my sisters. Now everyone will know and for that reason, I really struggled with the idea of including this in my book, but it is part of our lives.

With the Supreme Court overturning Roe vs Wade, I feel a need to tell this part of my life. I think of this every year when that date comes around and I always wonder who that person might have been. I did not realize that one day I would find someone who would know. One of my sisters likes going to "card readers" or clairvoyants so I went with her once while we were living in Texas in 2007. My sister went first, then waited in the parlor as I went in. As I sat down, an elderly lady with kind eyes asked for my hand. She looked at it intently and said, "You have three children." I quickly corrected her and said, "No, I only have two boys." Her next sentence left me bewildered and somewhat confused. I was not sure I truly believed in these folks and thought probably they just wanted your money. Her next statement confused me more.

"I see," she spoke. "She is okay now." I was stunned. How did she know? What did she mean? Had that child been a girl? And what did she mean by, "She is okay now?" I had my two sons by then, but one had SMA, that fatal genetic disorder. Did the clairvoyant's statement mean that she likely had SMA but was okay now, in heaven in a healthy body? I did not ask her to elaborate. Why? Because I will always wonder what life may have been like if we had that child. Would our marriage have survived? Would we have been strong enough to accept the diagnosis and commit like we did eight years later after we had one healthy child? There are times when I think that maybe that is the way our life was supposed to happen. None of these "what ifs" will ever make me feel better about our decision, but if things were meant to happen as they did, I was so glad to have Ian, our healthy baby boy born two years after we married. He would be the most amazing big brother to Jeremy. This is certainly not meant to justify our decision. It just makes me realize that we are not in control of our lives sometimes. We make decisions and do things that we may regret later, but life is never easy. My hope is that if she had SMA, that she and Jeremy are united in heaven now, each in a healthy body. Life happens...

We lived in Houston for one year and returned to California as a married couple, ready to take on the world and unaware of our future challenges. We settled into life in a small community in the Northern California foothills. Wayne returned to school, and I worked as an LVN at the local hospital. My goals for becoming an RN had not changed. We just needed to figure out where we were going to make our home. I wanted children since I was almost out of my childbearing years, but Wayne did not seem too interested. We were both attending the local junior college. I was trying to get into the RN program and he was taking construction and drafting classes. Unfortunately, that year the college administration decided that building an Olympic-sized swimming pool was more important than keeping the RN program. I was devastated. Wayne and I sat in the cafeteria as I cried and said, "I am never going to get into an RN program." To console me, my wonderful husband said, "If you're not going to get into a program anytime soon, maybe we can think about having a baby." What? What? When do we start? It only took three months to have a positive pregnancy test. This one was planned and on December 11, 1979, our son Ian was born. I worked that evening since my due date was not until the 24th, Christmas Eve, but Ian was not waiting till Christmas for us to open our presents. He was ready to join the family two weeks before his due date. I was working a 3-11 shift and was in labor during my shift but did not know it. Wayne picked me up at 11:30pm, brought me back at midnight and Ian was born at 4:14am.

Eighteen months later, I got into the RN program at American River College, where we had met. After 12 months of a very compressed intensive program to move from LVN to RN, I graduated in June 1982. My salary changed dramatically in the move from LVN to a registered nurse. As most new nurses do, I started out on the graveyard shift, which is good for learning new procedures and accepting more responsibility. We were then ready to purchase our first home, and we did. My first job as an RN was beginning.

Wayne, Ian, and I at his parent's home in Arkansas.

At that time, I met an outstanding nurse who would become my "surrogate" mom from that day to present. I remember being afraid to work nights because she was in charge. Everyone seemed to think that she was so mean. Now I think that was just a façade. She really had a heart of gold and was only mean to lazy nurses. I realized that if you did your job, cared for your patients and were productive, there was no need to be "talked to" by the charge nurse. She would later volunteer to come every Monday night, on her night off, to stay up all night with Jeremy. Who does that? God only made one of Mare, as Jeremy used to call her, since he could not say Marilyn. It was the only night of the week that we could sleep all night and know that Jeremy was in good hands.

My friend and surrogate mom, lovingly known as Mare.

We settled into our new home on Village Lane and soon met our neighbors across the street. We did not know it then, but Chris would become a significant part of our lives in regard to the loss of our son.

Chapter Nine
Adding to Our Family

When Ian was five, we decided that a sister or brother would be nice. I was doing well in my new position. The homes in our neighborhood had been officers' quarters when there was an active Army base in the community. Ours was a basic three-bedroom, one bath home with a single car garage. Since we were growing our family and Wayne had a wealth of remodeling experience, we made a plan to remodel. We decided to change the flat roof to a pitched roof and create an attic. Our new neighbors across the street were interested in having the same thing done. We became good friends and soon found out that we were both pregnant. My baby was due first. We wanted a girl but would take whatever we got as long as he or she was healthy. My gynecologist wanted me to have amniocentesis since I was going to be 36 when I delivered. I chose not to have that done. I remember telling him distinctly, "I do not want to have that because what if something is wrong with the baby? I will have to make a decision whether to continue the pregnancy or not. I do not want to make that decision, so I will take whatever I get." We had already made a decision like that, and we did not want to go through that again. The next sentence will haunt me forever. "I don't care if he is in a wheelchair and can't walk, as long as he has his brain, I will take him." Life happens…

Ian, age 5, with Jeremy, 24 hours old.

Our second son Jeremy was born on February 5, 1985. He was a beautiful child! He had all his fingers and toes and a beautiful smile. We would find out later that he was not perfect by any means. Our lives would change dramatically and our love and commitment to our marriage would be tested.

There were several things that happened to let me know that something was wrong, but I tried to ignore them. I was comparing him to my oldest son and kids do things differently. By the time Jeremy was 6 months old and did not move from any spot I placed him, I knew something was horribly wrong. My pediatrician referred us to a neurologist who suggested a muscle biopsy be done for better diagnoses. The day he called me at work to ask Wayne and me to come to his office to discuss findings was the worst day of my life. As we sat in his office, I could hear him flipping pages in a book in the back. I thought to myself, "Whatever it is, it must be rare because he is looking it up in his books." The statement that came next will be burned in my memory forever.

"Your son has Werdnig-Hoffmann Syndrome or spinal muscular atrophy. It is a recessive gene that both of you have. The lifespan for a Type I SMA is 18 months to 2 years."

What? Why? I remember coming home and looking it up in my pediatric nursing book. There was a small paragraph: "Werdnig-Hoffmann Syndrome is a disorder of the neuromuscular system which consists of atrophy of the anterior horn cells in the spinal cord and motor nuclei in the brainstem... As the disease progresses, swallowing becomes impossible and death results from aspiration and overwhelming infection. There is no cure, only supportive measures."

Due to the gravity of the diagnosis, we were referred to the Muscular Dystrophy Association clinic in San Francisco for a second opinion. They concurred, but they were very progressive and did not believe in putting a timeline on life expectancy. We felt more encouraged when we left that day, but the bottom line was that our son was never going to walk; he would spend whatever life he had in a wheelchair. Often, these SMA kids are brilliant. Wasn't that what I had asked for? I knew God would not be so cruel! There must be a reason. We would continue to follow up with the clinic until he became 18.

Werdnig-Hoffmann Syndrome affects the anterior horn cells in the spinal cord. The anterior horn cell sends impulses through motor neurons to make your muscles move. Without muscle movement, Jeremy would be unable to breathe and would die from respiratory failure.

At some point we realized that protecting our son did not mean keeping the truth from him. After he turned 18 and we visited the clinic, the pediatric neurologist asked our son if he had an advance directive. I was stunned. We had not spoken to him about any of this. He also informed Jeremy that even though medical research was working hard to find a cure, it was likely "not going to happen in your lifetime." Needless to say, the 2-hour ride home after that particular clinic day was emotionally draining. We had never discussed the fact that he would die. He had accepted the fact that he would not ever walk. But as usual, Jeremy was the adult in all this. We talked about it and did the advance directive. He knew exactly what his wishes were, and so we continued on. Life happens...

At our first clinic visit, all disciplines involved in the patient's care took their turn coming in to introduce themselves and offer information related to their field of expertise. The physical therapists came in and discussed range of motion exercises to decrease the inevitable contractures of his limbs. The nutritionist discussed his nutrition. Lastly, the social worker came in. After introducing herself, she proceeded to tell us that "80-85 percent of fathers leave the family when this happens. It is a difficult situation for a man, since he is supposed to fix things and make things better, and he cannot in this case. The family falls apart because the mother will spend all her time with the ill child and everyone else will be ignored." Personally, I felt that although that may have been true, it was not the right time to say that to us. Wayne practically lunged across the table at her saying, "Don't you put me in that category! I married my wife for better or worse and if this is the worse, then the better is coming. Don't you ever put me in that category! I am not leaving!" I was so proud of him and so was our son. The general consensus at that clinic was that they would not put a time frame on Jeremy's life and would assist us in doing whatever we could to give him the best possible quality of life. Dad, mom, and brother would work together to provide that for our baby. Our lives had changed but our commitment as a family would not waiver. The fight had begun!! Life happens...

We would not be defeated by this horrible disease. The decision was made. While we would provide the best quality of life that we could for Jeremy, we would not forget Ian. The family had to survive not only for

Jeremy but especially for Ian. We had to be sure that Ian's life was also as normal as possible. Soon after the diagnosis, Ian developed some behaviors at school. We met with a school psychologist and enrolled him in a "special friend" program that the school provided. He would meet with his friend during the week for art therapy to help him deal with emotions stemming from living with a chronically ill little brother and to help him understand as well as he could why Jeremy needed so much attention. That special friend really helped the boys develop the best relationship two brothers could have. I think that God gave us Ian because he knew he was going to give us Jeremy. I truly believe that Ian's relationship with his brother made the quality of his life so much better.

Ian with his baby brother, Jeremy

Ian and Jeremy

When Jeremy was 18 months old, he developed pneumonia and was placed on a ventilator so he could breathe. I remember the neurologist telling us that "he will die from pneumonia because he cannot manage his secretions." After two weeks in ICU, the doctors asked us to make that decision, to remove the vent and let him go. We could not do that! As a nurse, I knew we were just prolonging the inevitable. However, I could not let my baby die, not just yet. Even though there was no known cure, maybe if he lived long enough, they would find one and save him. In my heart, I knew that was not possible. They had not even identified the gene that caused the abnormality in the motor neuron cell. They would not have been able to identify the problem with an amniocentesis at the time I was pregnant. Our only other option was to place a tracheostomy tube in his throat to better ventilate his lungs. They were able to do that, and we took him home knowing that once again, life as we knew it had changed forever. Life happens…

We had a babysitter who watched both our sons, but once Jeremy came home with a trach, she was not able to care for him. This started a whole new problem. Would I have to quit work to care for him full-time? I had insurance through work for the whole family, including Jeremy. The hospital where I worked was wonderful. The administrative department, my manager, human resources, and my union worked together to get our insurance company to pay for an LVN to come in 5 days a week for 10 hours a day to care for him while I went to work. That was unheard of for any insurance company to do that. I felt so cared for by the organization I worked for because they were willing to do whatever it took to get our son covered so that I could continue to work for them. This was a small, fewer than 100-bed hospital on 26 acres of land that five doctors had mortgaged their homes to build. It seemed like the community was coming together for our son.

We were lucky to get his first nurse, Suzie. Unfortunately, she only cared for him for a year before she moved out of state. Next came three nurses who loved and cared for Jeremy so much that we felt comfortable returning to a somewhat "normal" life.

These nurses also moved on, and the last group hired were not of the same quality we were used to.

Because we felt so strongly about the lack of quality in his care, we decided to give up the benefit nursing care we were so lucky to have had for years. Wayne took over his care in 2006. We were on our own now. The good thing was there was a program available to pay family caregivers to care for disabled family members. Due to Jeremy's severe disability and total care needs, Wayne was allowed the most hours possible. That income helped until we moved to Texas in 2007. However, the In-Home Supportive Services program in Texas was more limited in funds and unable to provide as many hours of care.

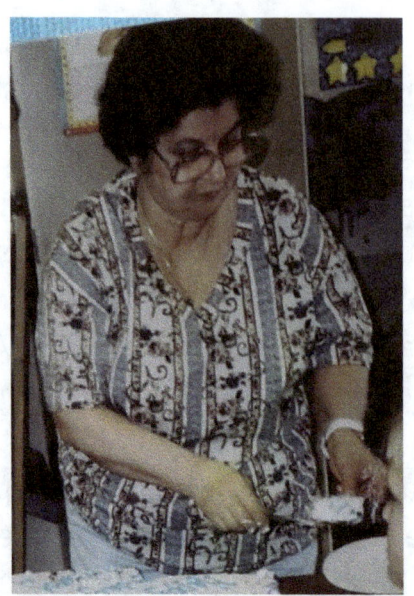

The "grandma" figure of Jeremy's nurses, Dottie. She was so great with him.

Best nurses, Cindy, and Joyce

In 1989, that small community hospital was bought out by a larger corporation. They were not eager to take on the responsibility of paying for our son to be cared for at home. It would cost many thousands of dollars a year, for equipment and nursing care. Jeremy was 4 years old at the time and had lived longer than we had anticipated. We had fought for his life from the beginning, and we were not going to stop now. When the medical director and other officials for the insurance company wanted to meet with us to discuss our options, we agreed. It just so happened that in that year, Jeremy had been selected as the ambassador of the Muscular Dystrophy Association (used to be called the poster child).

1989 Muscular Dystrophy Association Ambassador.

We arrived at the appointment to meet with people who were to determine whether or not our son deserved the quality of life we wanted to provide for him. Before the conversation even started, I pulled out the "poster child" picture of Jeremy and placed it in the middle of the round table we were all seated at. We went around the table and introduced ourselves as is customary. I do not think they were prepared for us to bring ammunition. I was so glad that I was a registered nurse and understood the totality of what the decisions made at this meeting would mean. The only way to maintain the quality of life that we were committed to providing for our son was to continue to receive the benefits that this corporation was reluctant to provide. The placement of our child in a nursing home was not an option. So, as we did when we had been given that dreadful diagnosis 4 years before, we dug in our heels and advocated for our son.

I started the meeting by introducing our son. "This is Jeremy Wayne Waggoner. He is a human being, not a medical record number or an account number on an insurance policy. We are all here today to discuss the continuation of his quality of life, as I hope we all agree." They were all a little stunned but reacted by saying, "Oh, he's so cute and, of course, that is our goal." However, they proceeded to discuss a variety of ways to get a nursing assistant to do the work instead of a licensed nurse. I kindly reminded them that our son was immobile and required medications, total care for eating and bathing, and suctioning of his trach to clear his airway. If they felt that a nursing assistant could legally perform all these functions and they were willing to take all liability for any unfavorable outcomes, then yes, an aide could care for him.

We left the meeting with a win. My employer would continue to provide a licensed vocational nurse 10 hours a day, five days a week. I wondered how some families with kids like ours where the parents had no knowledge of nursing, or the workings of the medical service made it through their tough lives. I prayed that a higher power was looking out for them. I was happy he was for us. The new company would provide the same amount of nursing care until the quality of nurses declined.

Our quest to provide our son with a life as close to normal as possible continued. Eventually he had a gastrostomy tube placed to provide better nutrition. Due to his extreme weakness, it was difficult for him to eat enough food to get the calories necessary to sustain him. Chewing and swallowing took too much energy. In between chewing and swallowing, he had to breathe; when given an option whether to eat or breathe, one can understand why he chose to breathe. So, at age 5, the tube was placed, and we could feed him through it while he slept. During the day, he would have "comfort food," things he enjoyed like pizza, angel hair pasta, and soups. He would eat very small amounts very carefully to avoid things going down the wrong way. Life happens...

When it was time for kindergarten, Jeremy was placed in a special education school in the next town over. His nurses always accompanied him because of his fragile medical condition. He needed medications and suctioning during the day. Although SMA kids cannot move, they are extremely smart. After a while, he became bored with the special education program. We took the next scary step and decided to "mainstream" him. That is when children with disabilities are placed in regular classrooms, into the mainstream, to socialize them with "regular" kids. It was scary in that there were only 8 kids in the special class, while a regular class could have up to 25 students. The thought of more kids with more germs to potentially infect our fragile son was something to consider.

Thus started a new chapter of advocating for our son. The special education student receives an IEP (Individual Educational Program) plan every year. The parents and educators of the child meet with administrative staff. The goal is to evaluate the student and his progress and set goals for the coming year. The special education program required that the student be provided a "scribe" to take notes or do any physical activity that the student was unable to do. The school did not want to provide a scribe because Jeremy had a nurse with him; they thought the nurse should act as scribe. They seemed more concerned about the expense of a scribe than with the health and education of our child. The supervisor for his nurses even attended the meeting to explain that her nurse's job was caring for our Jeremy's medical and physical needs, not being a teacher's aide. They finally accepted that fact and complied. However, there were times when "they could not find a scribe" and the nurse ended up taking notes for him. It was very difficult for us to believe that the "administrative" person drove a Mercedes Benz, but the district could not afford a scribe for our son.

We continued to integrate Jeremy into life with adjustments. The community had a program for children with disabilities, known as Challenger Baseball. The disabled child would have a "buddy" who would help with hitting the ball and pushing them around the bases. There were no outs, and everybody won. As it should be in life; sometimes children teach us the best lessons.

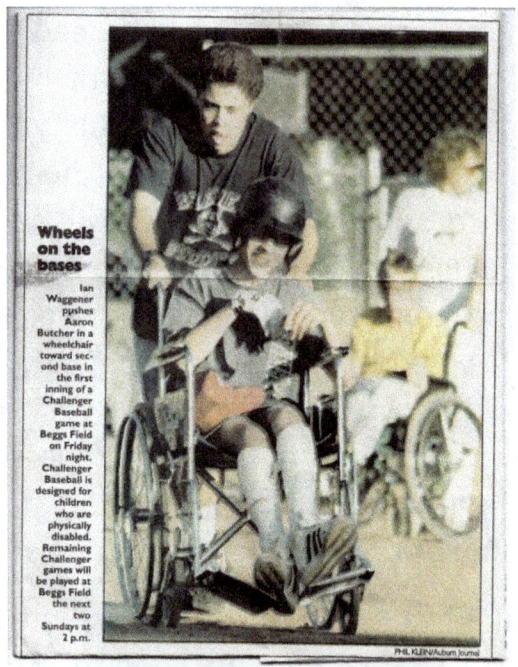

Ian pushing Aaron Butcher.

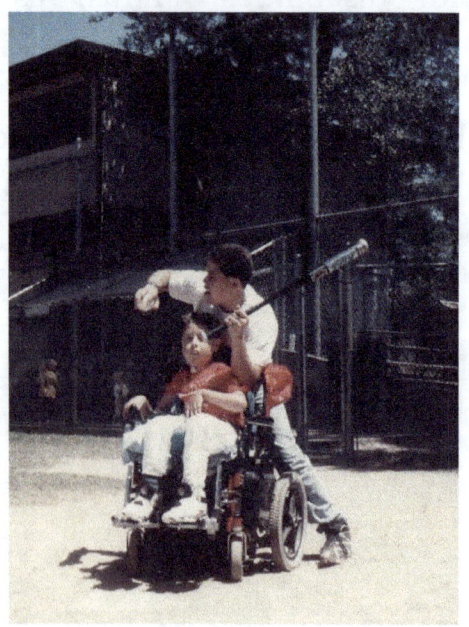

Jeremy with buddy Ian.

By the time he got to high school, Jeremy had become bored with school. Remember that SMA kids are smarter than normal, almost as if their brains work overtime since their bodies can't. At the end of his junior year, Jeremy said to me, "I am not going to school anymore." What? "I know, you think I need to go for the 'social' part of school. Why? I am not going to the prom. I do not care about my 'peers.' They only care about themselves. They are into their own things." It was as if he was saying, "Life is too short for me to care about these mundane things, I need to keep moving forward." Okay, he made his point. "But you can't just quit." Typical of Jeremy, he had thought this out. He would take his GED and go on to junior college. That he did, and with his nurse at his side, he attended the local junior college. He wanted to play basketball so badly but obviously, he could not. He decided to take classes to become a coach. We never told him he could not do anything, and always gave him an alternative way to do something. I remember the pain I felt in my heart, the first time he said, "When I am not in my wheelchair, then I can run and play basketball." My response was always, "But if you still need your wheelchair, then can we do it this way, in your chair." He was always so accepting. Life happens…

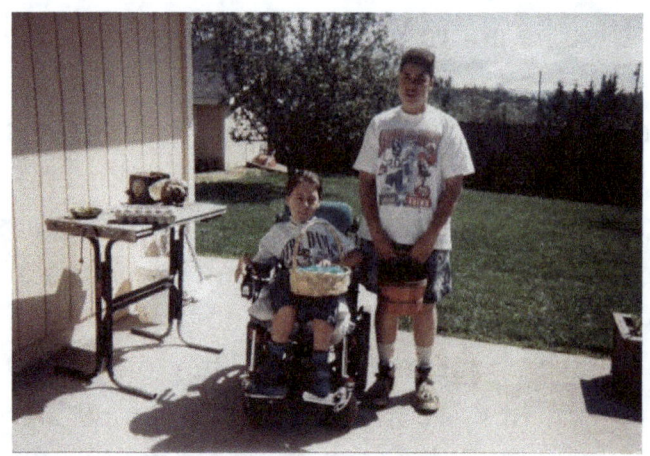

*Big brother, Ian, always helping.
Hunting for Easter eggs in our backyard.*

Brothers playing Battleship.

At age 10 Jeremy went through a very drastic back surgery to allow him to sit up better and breathe easier. He survived although it required 10 hours of surgery and 6 units of blood. Sometimes we questioned some of the procedures to make his life better since they were so invasive and brutal for such a fragile body. He was the bravest soul I ever knew. He never complained. We were always thinking of ways to help him participate in life with the best quality we could.

I realized how lucky I was to be a nurse and to have a loving husband who would be by me the entire journey until the end. Wayne's pain was just as great as mine and we would need each other to survive the future. Our oldest son would also need us, and we made sure he was not forgotten through all this. Ian eventually learned how to change Jeremy's trach and gastrostomy tubes. When I worked the evening shift, I was afraid that if tubes fell out, Wayne would not be able to handle it. I remember the conversation with Jeremy when I asked him if his big brother could learn how to change his tubes. He asked, "Why can't Dad do it?" My response, almost without thinking, was "It hurts Dad's heart to do it." Typical of a Jeremy response, "Oh, okay, yeah, Ian can do it." I felt comfortable leaving him home during my shift from 3pm to 11pm.

Ian volunteered at the hospital where I worked. The position was equivalent to "candy stripers." I was working on the evening he was scheduled to receive his "100 hours served" award. Wayne and Jeremy were home but were going to attend the ceremony, and I planned to take my dinner break at that time and attend with them. The ceremony was being held in one of the hospital's conference rooms. We waited for Wayne and Jeremy to arrive, but they did not. I called the house but no one answered, so the ceremony went on and I had my dinner.

They finally arrived, three hours later. The tale they told just breaks my heart every time I think about it. My husband, the man who would not give up on his family, who would eventually give up his career to care for our son, had been held at the house by a sheriff and child protection worker on a charge of "child neglect." With lights flashing, the sheriff pulled into our long driveway. Wayne could see it was a sheriff with a woman at the door. He thought they were asking for donations. When he answered the door, the child protective services worker stated, "We have a complaint about you." He let them in only to find out that it would become the worst evening possible.

The week before, we had dismissed one of the nurses because she was not very attentive to our son's needs. I had reported her to her supervisor and asked for her not to come back. Apparently, she was not happy about that. When Wayne asked, "Why are you here?" the worker stated someone had reported that drugs and alcohol were being used excessively where a disabled child lived. The report also stated that "unsavory characters with long hair" were hanging around our home all the time. We had one friend with very long hair who drove a Harley. The worker would not say who had made the report other than it was "a professional who was aware of the situation."

Apparently, because it was a professional, nothing was verified before the decision was made to terrorize my family. I figured it was the lazy nurse who also turned out to be vindictive. This was her way of getting back at us. The attack on Wayne's character continued for more than two hours. The large sheriff stood at the doorway with his hand on his gun, eventually making his way to stand behind Wayne, as the worker verbally abused him. I guess he was ready in case Wayne attacked the indignant person in front of him. When they entered our home, the worker stated, "Well, this is the first time we have done this in a home this nice." We had just moved into our new home and neighborhood two weeks before. Jeremy presented himself, in his wheelchair, well-kept and in an obviously loving home, yet the attack went on. Jeremy was not being abused by anyone other than by them. They scared him by threatening to take him away from us. When they realized the extent of his care and that no one else would be able to care for him, they finally started to ease up. They would have likely put him in a nursing home where his quality of life would have ceased to exist.

I was so angry when I realized what had happened. How dare they accuse my husband of abusing our child! This was the man who vowed not to be part of that statistic of 85% of men leaving the marriage. I proceeded to write a letter to the Child Protective Services of Placer County to express my disappointment in the way the situation was handled. I felt that they owed my husband and son an apology for brutalizing them for over two hours in our home. To this day, my husband suffers from PTSD from that whole incident. Those two people who came to our home and terrorized our family were able to go home and enjoy their lives without understanding the trauma they had inflicted. It has been 30 years since that incident and it still makes me so angry. I realize the agency is there to help keep children safe. As soon as they arrived and saw the beautiful home and great care for our son plus no drugs or alcohol, I feel it should have ended right there. I will remember it forever, and my heart still hurts for my husband who endured that abuse and never received an apology. Life happens…and sometimes it sucks!!

The Waggoners in Auburn with dog, Charlie.

Life Happens, Keep Moving Forward

Chapter Ten
Career Changes and Surviving Cancer

My career was progressing and eventually, I received my bachelor's degree in nursing. I was offered a management position in the rehabilitation unit and the new skilled nursing unit down the hall from the surgical unit where I was a charge nurse. I accepted and began to learn a new type of nursing. Acute rehab included patients who had experienced a traumatic event, such as a stroke or a head or spinal cord injury. The skilled side cared for the elderly or folks who just needed very short rehab before they could return home. I was looking forward to my new adventure. Jeremy's condition seemed to stabilize, especially after the surgery to help him sit up straighter and breathe easier. I did not realize it at that time, but life was going to throw us more challenges.

In November 2003, while preparing to open the new skilled nursing unit, I received the results of a recent mammogram and subsequent biopsy. It was positive for breast cancer. I was shocked but knew that I had a fight on my hands. As a nurse, I wondered why women would choose a lumpectomy rather than mastectomy. "Just take the breast off, it's diseased." But when it was my turn, I also chose to have a lumpectomy first. Unfortunately, when the specimen edges are "dirty," that means they did not get it all. The question becomes, "Do I continue to cut away at the tissue and hope to get it all or do I remove it all?" In January 2004, I had surgery to remove my right breast and followed by reconstruction and chemotherapy. After four rounds of heavy-duty chemo and all my hair falling out, I beat it! My hair began to fall out after the second round. I cried, only to have Jeremy tell me, "Come on, let's go to your stylist and we can shave our hair off." That was a bad day made good. He had that ability.

Me, after chemo treatments.

My greatest fear was not of dying but of not being there for our son. It was my work insurance that covered all his medical needs. I couldn't die now. Although I tried not to think about it, the thought came creeping up in my head.

What did I always want for myself? If I was going to die, I was going to oblige myself. I went down to the local used car dealer and bought a 1998 BMW 528i. It still had a warranty, and I had my Beamer. It was a little hard to explain to my husband when I drove up to his job site in my new car. After checking it over and kicking the tires a little, he said, "Well, okay." Just another example of the wonderful person I married. I had that car for a while until a crazy person came out the wrong way and drove across my path. I hit him and totaled my car. He got away. Fortunately, the insurance company paid me what it was worth. It was more than I owed, so I got myself a BMW X3 SUV. I had come a long way from my 1966 Plymouth Valiant.

After my mastectomy, an annual mammogram became more and more frightening. Most women worry about having their breasts squashed down like a pancake to get a good image. I worried about what that image would show. This was another bump in the road for our family, one that would add to our daily stress of caring for a terminally ill child. However, with complete trust in our family, we forged ahead. We were too strong as a family to let anything keep us from maintaining a great quality of life for us and especially for Jeremy. He was approaching his 21st birthday in a couple of years and it would be quite a celebration. That was a long way from his 18 months to 2 years prognosis.

Jeremy knew we were always willing to do whatever it took for his quality of life, so when I asked him what he wanted for his 21st birthday, expecting an answer like, "a PlayStation game," he surprised me with. "I don't want to be a virgin anymore!" Okay, that set me back a few years! It was not an unreasonable request, but how does that happen when the person is unable to move? Call in the experts, the ladies with the oldest profession. It's illegal in California, but Nevada is right next door with all kinds of things that are legal. The question was how to get him into that situation. Nursing gives you very good problem-solving skills. The problem would be keeping his breathing from being compromised during this strenuous event. Our oldest son and his friends did some research and found a place where he would be safe. We would just have to trust that everything would go well.

On Memorial Day weekend 2006, Wayne and I left for Colorado to visit family while the kids prepared to help Jeremy experience life. A hotel in Las Vegas provided the lodging with all necessities to allow for the use of a ventilator, feeding tube machines, suction machines, and breathing treatments to keep him safe.

When we got back from Colorado, I remember saying to Jeremy, "Without giving me any details, how did things go in Nevada?" He smiled and said, "Mom, that lady knew exactly what to do." Because he had absolutely no muscles at all, he was not able to move by himself. He had to be lifted out of his wheelchair into the bathtub, on the toilet, etc. He was completely dependent on all his care. However, normal sexual development occurred with absolutely no way to release any of his physical needs. I always used to think, "he was not able to be a normal teen male and help himself." He could not move! Some folks may think it's weird to do this for your son but when we made a commitment to give him the best quality of life possible, we were not kidding. Sex is part of life. We were glad to help him experience it. Life happens...

The following year, things started changing at my job. My position was eliminated, and Jeremy got so sick that we thought he may succumb to the disease. We had bought property in Texas and made a critical decision to build our dream home and move there. We would be closer to my family and if we lost our son, the support would be there. Unfortunately, things didn't work out that way. Our home was beautiful, the environment was so different, and my new job was not very rewarding. Eventually, I was asked to leave because I "did not follow their values." I was a very committed rehabilitation nurse who was uncomfortable working in a hospital that did not value its employees and did not care about patient safety. Yes, my values were different. I valued my employees, and patient safety was of utmost importance. I could not work in a place with such different values. The odd thing was that this organization was faith-based. I realized that we had made a terrible mistake. Even trying to live in my old state at other times never worked. Life happens...

Before we moved to Texas, Jeremy was getting involved with a group of boys around Ian's age who had a band. A young man named Jaydon would become one of Jeremy's best friends and eventually one of his caregivers. They gave Jeremy a snare drum for his birthday and attached it to his wheelchair so that he could play it. He was also able to play a small guitar. His dad made him a pick with a dowel stick so that he could pick at the strings. I was sad to leave California at a time when he was doing something he loved, but we had already made a financial commitment and there was no turning back. Two of Jeremy's friends from the band rode with us out to Texas to help us move and have one last time with their friend. Jaydon would later come to Texas to help with his care while we waited to sell our dream home and return to California.

Jeremy wrote two books of prose and poetry, and Jaydon helped with the writing and printing of the books. Eventually, copies would be sold, and money donated to CureSMA. To this day, I have not been able to completely read either of the books, since they tell of his raw feelings about his life and situation. He was not bitter, but accepted his situation and the fact that his life on this earth was limited and he had to get as much out of life as he could.

Even with his limited mobility, he was able to draw and play guitar and drums with some alterations. He enjoyed drawing Disney cartoons freehand.

Jeremy's painting. I'm amazed how he could control his movements to stay within the lines.

Some of Jeremy's artwork that we gave to our dear friend, Mare, who sat with him on Monday nights.

He enjoyed doing many other things with creative modifications. At his side awaiting instructions, I would place that Velcro strip just so on his overbed table for him to build with Legos. The Legos with the ability to turn up and down were the best. He would add extensions to the controllers on the Legos so that he could reach them just enough to make them perform their function. The Velcro kept the newly developed extended controller from moving! He actually drew plans to develop controllers on his CAD computer at school, but he never tried to pitch his idea to the gaming companies.

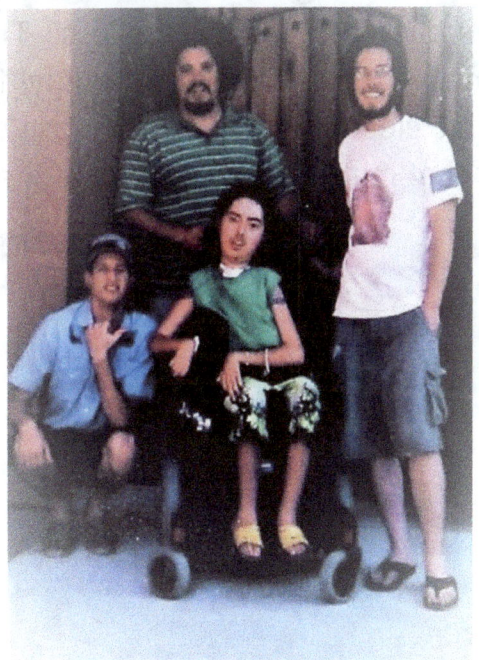

Ian behind Jeremy, Jaydon (standing), and Jordan (kneeling).

We had built our dream home on an acre of beautiful land close to the water in Ingleside, Texas. My husband had designed the beautiful 3100 square foot home, all handicapped accessible with an awesome room for Jeremy. The contractor went over budget by $42,000 but failed to tell us until the day we were supposed to move in, putting us in a real bind. We had a family coming for an open house, and we needed to get out of the hotel where we were living. We accepted and moved in.

The president of the Texas bank that had financed our project was now telling us, "If you don't like it, just sell it!" Were people really that heartless? This was our dream home. Our son was terminally ill. We just wanted to live close to our family in case we lost him. But none of that mattered, and they got their money.

The front of our dream home in Texas.

Our Texas home with a veranda in the back.

Then 18 months later, I lost my job. Something told me it was time to head back to California. Jeremy's fear was that he would get very sick and no one at the hospital would know what to do. "Mom, if I get sick, put me on a plane and send me back to Dr. Chipps in Sacramento. These people will kill me here."

Chapter Eleven
Returning Home

In California in October 2009, Ian and Deidra got married. Jeremy was his brother's best man.

Ian and Deidra's wedding in Folsom with Jeremy as best man.

While we were there, I applied for a rehab nursing job with a local faith-based hospital and was hired immediately. We returned to Texas, and I packed my bags and drove my Beamer back to California, leaving my husband and son in Texas by themselves to sell our dream home and join me as soon as possible. Six months later, I returned to Texas to bring Jeremy back to California. We lived with Ian and Deidra until Wayne was able to join us. In March 2011, McKinsey was born and I quickly moved into the role of Grandma.

McKinsey and Grandma Waggoner

We all lived in a small rental house until we could build our last and permanent home. Of course, the design had to be handicapped-accessible and at ground level. However, before we could do that, we would have to find an accessible apartment. We needed to start looking immediately so I had this conversation with Ian.

Me: "We are looking for a handicapped-accessible apartment so we can move and give you and your family your own space."

Ian: "You know that Jeremy is not going with you."

Me: "What? He has to. He is our responsibility."

Ian: "You and Dad have done enough. It is my turn to take care of him. You and Dad need to go off and start your marriage."

Me: "But you guys just had a baby and what does your wife think?"

Ian: "She feels the same way. She loves him just as much as we do."

With tears in my eyes, I hugged him and realized that we had raised a beautiful human being who had the same compassion and love for his brother that we did. And apparently, so did his wife. It was the best two years of his life. He was finally independent of his parents. He had always wanted us to get him a permanent caregiver so he could live in his own apartment. We could never trust anyone to care for him like we did. The move with his brother was the best thing we did. It allowed Jeremy to develop a beautiful relationship with his niece. She was three when he passed but she still remembers him.

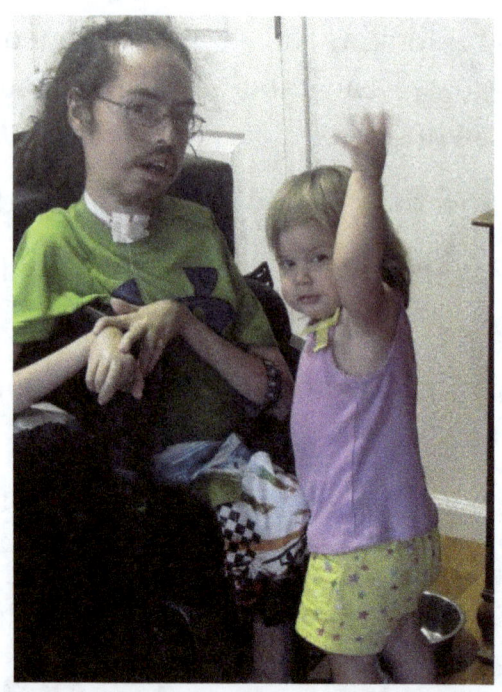

McKinsey enjoying a ride with Uncle Jeremy.

She loved getting rides in his wheelchair and was always there to hand Dad or Grandpa whatever was needed for his care.

Jeremy and McKinsey at their home in Lincoln, 2014.

I remember teaching Ian how to change the tracheostomy tube or the feeding tube on his little brother when Ian was only 8 years old. Years later, Ian ended up using those skills. Towards the end of Jeremy's life, round-the-clock care was provided by his dad and brother. I am so proud of my husband for living by the words of his commitment to his wife and family, "for better, for worse." I remember his reaction when the social worker recited the statistics of fathers leaving the family because they could not fix the problem. Yes, we could not fix the problem, but we could work together to give our son a great quality of life. We accomplished that by keeping our family intact.

Since the goal was always to provide Jeremy with as much of a "normal" life as possible, when we found out that Ziggy Marley was playing at a nearby Indian casino, we immediately got tickets for September 8, 2012. What Jeremy did not know was that I had arranged with the entertainment manager for Jeremy to meet Ziggy. It was quite a feat. We saw the show and then surprised Jeremy by telling him at the last minute that he was going to go meet Ziggy. It almost literally took his breath away. He was so excited! He looked at me and asked, "Ma, how did you do this?" My one and only answer for him was, "I would move mountains for you, sweetie!"

Chapter Twelve
And Then the Angels Came

Jeremy loved Bob Marley and reggae. He wore dreadlocks; the longest one was 30 inches long. Sundays were mine for his care. I knew the drill with the dreads, washing and twisting just right, adding the shea butter.

Surprise visit with Ziggy Marley at Cache Creek Casino.

The Sunday of the week he passed, I saw that familiar look that I saw in my terminally ill patients when they were ready to go. As I stood behind him, twisting his dreads, I said to my son what I said to my patients when I saw "the look."

"Jeremy, you do not have to do this anymore if you can't. It is okay. We will be okay." It's called, "giving your patient permission to die." He was gone in the early morning on Thursday of that week.

It was January 30, 2014, noon at work and I was just sitting down to lunch. One bite into my sandwich and my phone rang. It was Wayne. He had arrived at 7am to take over Jeremy's care while Ian rested before going to his other job. I was so glad that Ian had been sitting at his bedside when he passed.

We would find out that Jeremy died in his sleep between 3-4 in the morning. The ventilator continued to give him breaths and his feeding continued. I left work hoping that Wayne's call urging me to come to Jeremy's "right now and drive safely" was not the call I had been dreading. The thought that kept running through my mind was, "Please let it be just an issue with equipment or his tubes and please God, I do not want to see the coroner in the driveway."

Unfortunately, the coroner was there. Jeremy was 28 years, 11 months, and 25 days old (6 days away from his 29th birthday), having far outlived his prognosis. He had been gone for a few hours before we realized it. Sadly, this day would haunt his father forever.

Although there was nothing Wayne could have done to save him, as a father, he felt that he should have tried. I was reminded of the social worker's statement years before, that a father's innate responsibility to care for his family and keep them safe would eventually cause most fathers to leave. Not Wayne, not Jeremy's dad. He stayed and saved him for almost 29 years. I am so proud of him for that.

We had planned a trip to Jamaica for Jeremy's 30th birthday the following year. He really wanted to go to Hawaii, but we convinced him Jamaica would be better since traveling there did not require an airplane flight. We had a bad experience with flying when he was younger because of his medical needs. We could drive to Texas and board a cruise ship in Galveston. That would ensure that all his medical equipment, motorized wheelchair, and medical supplies would be with us and not with the baggage handlers. So, the plans were made to go to Jamaica, not knowing how we would transport him once we got there. Jeremy agreed since we might be able to visit Bob Marley's grave. Our travel agent suggested getting travel insurance in case anything came up. I agreed since he could be sick at travel time and we might have to cancel. Never did I think he could be gone. We were able to change our travel plans to Hawaii the following year. This was even better since it was where he wanted to go originally.

I never learned how to swim and I am afraid of heights. When we were planning our cruise, my conversation with Jeremy was that I would try ziplining and snorkeling on our trip. "Yeah, right," was his response. The following year at the time he would have been 30, we left for Hawaii. Ian and Deidra came with us, and I took some of Jeremy's ashes to leave in Hawaii. In order to do what I had promised Jeremy, we scheduled those two excursions plus a volcano trip.

As we were unloading at our rental, a single yellow butterfly flew by, hovered a little, then moved away. I did not think much about it since we were on a tropical island. The following day, we headed to the zipline place where we had reservations. We arrived a little early, so we wandered around the area, exploring. A single yellow butterfly hovered, then left. Again, I did not think much about it. But a few days later, as we prepared to go snorkeling, here comes that single yellow butterfly again, same maneuver. No one else saw it but me and as one would expect, they were a little skeptical. Nonetheless, I felt it was Jeremy letting me know he was proud of me. It has been 8 years since he passed but I still receive visits from my single yellow butterfly. He continues to watch over me.

Recently, I had a yellow butterfly tattooed on my left lower leg. He was always the "wings beneath my feet."

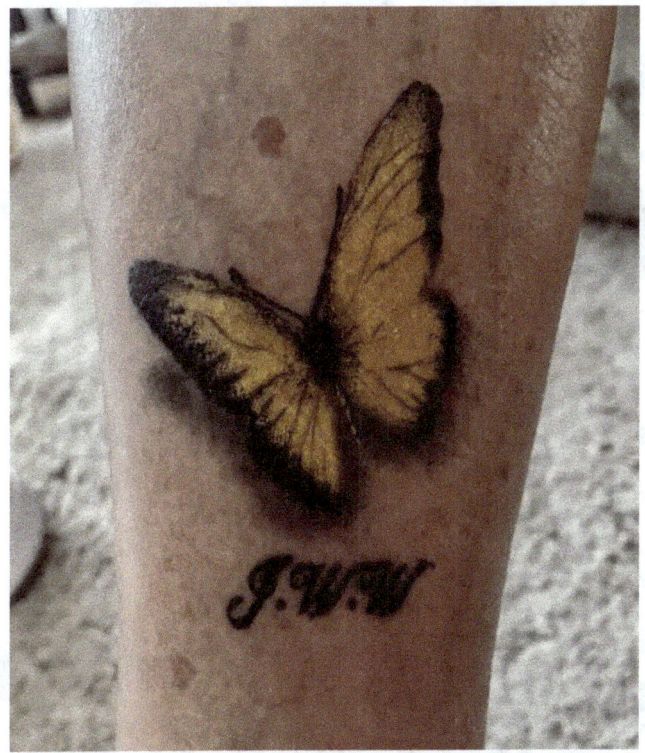

Tattoo by Brady Alberts at Syndicate Tattoos, Auburn, CA.

Ziplining for Jeremy.

Snorkeling for Jeremy

Chapter Thirteen
Reassuring Family is Okay

Some people will just simply not believe what follows, but I choose to believe because of my spiritual upbringing and my belief that there is a wonderful place called heaven. When we bought our first home in 1983, we became good friends with the family across the street. Chris and I were pregnant at the same time; I was hoping for a girl since we already had a 5-year-old son. Their girl and our boy were born within three months of each other. Their baby progressed to walking and running, ours did not. Once we settled into our diagnosis and what we had to do to survive as a family, we focused on meeting any and all challenges. We moved away to a new area and did not have much contact with my old friend and neighbor.

What I did not know was that Chris would end up being a huge help to me in dealing with Jeremy's death. You see, my dear friend is a clairvoyant. What is that, you ask? It is a person with the supposed ability to see things that are not in sight or cannot be seen by others. This will make sense later in this story.

Jeremy and I were very close in that I could speak to him frankly about his condition. He was wise beyond his years. In fact, I would always accuse him of being the "adult in the house." I suppose it was because he realized his life was short, so he was more open and honest about his feelings. He would say to me, "Madre (I loved that he called me that), don't worry when I am gone. I had a life before this one and I will have another after." I could somewhat understand his way of accepting his life, as he could not change it. He was a wise man in a crumpled, twisted little body who knew so much more about life than we did.

After giving him "permission to leave," I realized that we had never discussed how he was going to "come back and let me know he was okay" once he was gone. So, in the days and weeks after he passed, I cried a lot and, in my anguish, I talked to Jeremy about it. I had notified friends and family almost immediately after he passed and had received many calls and cards, but we had not heard from our former neighbor and friend Chris. I called her to let her know the date and time of the memorial, and I will never forget what she said when she answered the phone.

"I can't talk to you right now. I will call you back in 20 minutes. I have spoken to Jeremy." Thus began the longest 20 minutes of my life; almost like the 20-minute drive from work to Jeremy and Ian's house that dreadful day.

"What do you mean, you spoke to Jeremy?" I thought. Until then I had forgotten that she was clairvoyant. I began to remember stories she had told me years ago while we were neighbors, of different incidents when she was able to speak to a spirit and help them cross over. At this point, we had not been neighbors for 13 years. She had not seen or spoken with Jeremy since we had left for Texas in 2007. She did not know what his plans were or what he always wanted to do if he could walk. Now, in 2014, he had visited her because his Madre was crying too much and he needed to let her know he is okay.

Chris finally called me back and explained. He came to me and said that we had to call you right now.

Their conversation went like this:

Jeremy: "She does not know that I am okay, so I have to let her know."

Chris: "But it's 2am, she is sleeping right now."

Jeremy: "It doesn't matter, she needs to know that I am okay so she can stop crying."

Chris: "What happened to you? Your father is so upset because he did not know you were gone."

Jeremy: "Tell Dad I was gone long before he got there."

The coroner said Jeremy passed between 3:00 and 4:00am, and his dad had arrived at 7am. Ian was at his bedside. Normally, Ian would go to bed after getting Jeremy all set up but this night, he stayed in the recliner next to Jeremy's bed. His brother had been at his bedside when the angels came. I was glad to know that

Jeremy had not been alone. It's said that a mother knows when something has happened to her child, but I truly do not remember feeling any different that morning when I got up to get ready for work. Sometimes, I wish I could remember but it makes no difference. He was gone.

Jeremy proceeded to tell Chris what had happened. His brother put him to bed as usual, providing breathing treatments, administering his medications, and tube feeding. That night Ian added a little beer per request. He quietly went to sleep as the mechanical ventilator delivered breaths and oxygen through his tracheostomy tube in the throat. As he slept, two boys named Pete and Joe came to visit. Jeremy tells my friend that he knew them from "another life" and he knew they were dead. We did not know Pete or Joe, but I remember him telling me he had "another life before this one." The boys told him it was time to go and that he needed to go with them. He could not say how they got where they were going, but he said that when they arrived, they were greeted by many people, and they all were very happy. The boys asked what he wanted to do. I could have answered that for them. "I want to play basketball." The boys tell him that while he is there, he can have whatever body he wants. I was not surprised when I heard who he chose. No, not The Rock or Michael Jordan! He chose his brother's body. His brother weighed 235 pounds. Jeremy weighed 80 pounds. "Tell Ian that he isn't really fat, it's just his arms are so heavy. The boys had to help me with my new arms until I got used to them. Now I am running up and down the court and making 3 pointers."

My friend never knew that he always wanted to play basketball. Jeremy would have been the only one to tell her.

After two days, the boys tell him that he does not have to stay if he does not want to. They informed him that he can return to his former life and "do this some other time." The following statement hurts yet is truly understandable. "I looked down and saw myself on the ventilator and decided to stay. Tell my parents that they need to go on vacation wherever they want to go. They don't need to go to Jamaica. The other day, I saw Bob Marley at the park, and he was awesome!" Jeremy also wanted Chris to tell his father that he needed to get back into his artwork. Jeremy did not think it was a good idea for him to go to work as an activity coordinator in a nursing home. He knew that his dad cared too much about people and it would only make him sad if he was not able to help. His artwork would make him happier. Another side note: my friend did not know that Wayne had taken that course or was thinking of working in a nursing home. Only Jeremy could have told her that. I am happy to say that Wayne is very actively working on his artwork and has produced some beautiful watercolor paintings. Jeremy knew art would be therapeutic and help him heal. He started by finishing the project he had begun years earlier at the start of our journey. He would paint several amazing watercolors in the years to come. Life happens...

Wayne started this watercolor in the late 90's but it was set aside because it took a lot of attention. Because of Jeremy's prodding, he finally completed it after Jeremy's death.

Wayne's donation to a local art gallery.

Wayne's donation to fundraiser

One of many lighthouse paintings that Wayne created.

We had planned the trip to Jamaica for Jeremy's 30th birthday. Chris did not know about any of our travel plans. The only one who could have told her was Jeremy.

As of this writing, he has not visited Chris again, and I suppose that his soul is at rest now since he was able to get his message to me. I do cry less, knowing that he is in heaven in a pain-free body, enjoying the game he loved.

There were two other times he appeared while he was settling things. He was very close to his cousin, Amaris, in Texas and he visited her in a dream. It was two days after he passed and, in her dream, he was sitting across from her trying to say something to her. She could not understand him but he kept pointing at his body and trying to say something. What she noticed was that it was Jeremy's face with his dreads, but he had this "really huge body." This was two days after the boys in heaven had given him "Ian's body."

On the night he passed, my older sister, Mary, dreamed that she was at our farm where we all grew up. She was walking towards the house and my parents were there. My mother was walking towards her telling her, "Look, it's Fidela's baby. He is so happy. He is running around playing and having fun." She responded by saying that my baby cannot run. He is in a wheelchair. My mother said, "No, he is here, and he is so happy. He is running and playing." She woke up and got the call that he had passed. My parents have been in heaven for a very long time. It made me happy to know that they are together and finally got to meet.

We were lucky to have our son for longer than the known prognosis. Since his passing, research scientists have developed a treatment for Spinal Muscular Atrophy, not a cure, but I am sure that is on the horizon.

Current treatments can stop or slow down the progression of the disease, allowing for a longer life of better quality.

For some of us, the journey has stopped, and the healing is in progress. We continue to be active in fundraising for Families of SMA with the ultimate goal of a cure for this horrific disease that takes so many young lives. Jeremy's legacy is to educate people about the condition and encourage people to support their local SMA chapter.

His motto was "Love is My Religion." Donate to CureSMA.org.

Chapter Fourteen
Continuing to Fight

In 2016, I finally retired from nursing. I had put in my time, and I did not have to work so hard anymore. I did not need that insurance that had helped to care for our son for so long. It was time to start enjoying life and making time for ourselves.

Ian and Deidra were doing well. McKinsey is growing up too quickly. My new role is as a grandma and not a caregiver. We had awaited and feared the day when we would not have Jeremy anymore. Every year that we celebrated another birthday, I would let out a little of the breath I had been holding from the time I heard, "Your son will not survive past 18 months to 2 years." Now I could take a deep breath and know that our boy was living the life he was meant to have. We just would have to learn how to continue our life without him.

The question now was, "Where do we go from here?" We had been on a mission to prolong his life and its quality, knowing that we would eventually have to stop. I always dreaded the day that we would have to make that decision. I would run scenarios through my mind. How would he leave us? The scenario I hated the most was the one when he would become so sick that we would have to take him to the hospital. Days would pass and once again the medical team would come to us with that question. How long do we go on? When do you "pull the plug?" We did not have to make that decision like we did when he was 18 months old and we had elected to place a tracheostomy tube instead of letting him go. Because we had completed an Advance Directive when he turned 18, we knew what Jeremy wanted. As it turned out, it happened just like he planned, I am sure. He was always concerned about us and our well-being, so he just went to sleep and drifted to heaven while his brother was at his bedside. He had relieved us of our duties. We did not have to make a decision. He had decided himself. He had so little control, but he could make this decision on his own and at his own time. It is difficult for his father to accept that he was not able to help him in the end. But I am sure that Jeremy would say to him, "Dad, life is always happening; you just have to keep moving forward."

So how does one keep moving forward when life has literally been sucked out of your family? We continue his legacy by being part of the organization whose goal is to find a cure for this horrific disease.

One of the last fundraisers in our backyard with his good friend, Jaydon.

We have started having fundraisers every year in August since it is National SMA Month. We did some while he was still alive and two more after. We generally raise $2000 from friends and family. We participate in fundraisers in the San Francisco Bay Area each year.

Jeremy wanted everyone to be educated about the disease he had. The more people know about it and know someone affected by it, the more likely they are to donate. We participated in the Muscular Dystrophy Association's yearly Labor Day Telethon which was emotionally draining for us. It wasn't until we became involved with the grassroots organization known as Families of SMA that we felt like we were making a difference. Spinal Muscular Atrophy was only one of 40 diseases that the MDA funds benefitted. Unfortunately, a lot of the funds are used for administrative costs and salaries for those who are not volunteers. The SMA organization uses all funds for research, so we concentrate on the local chapter.

Chapter Fifteen
Honoring Jeremy's Life
Through His Poetry

Life continues without our "golden child," as he liked to refer to himself. With the help of his friend Jaydon, he was able to put his thoughts and feelings into poetry. He had two books printed, not published, and I thought another way to honor him was to add some of his poetry to the last part of this story. His life only lasted 28 years, 11 months, and 25 days but he left a legacy second to none. These are some of his thoughts.

Jeremy in his living area in Texas home.

Equal Humanity

I've been driving down the road,
In my wheelchair
To places I don't know.
I look to my left,
I look to my right,
I look up at the sky
Into the sunlight.
What's around me, what do I see?
People who don't care
About equal humanity.

If this were the time of the Romans
I would be the Poor.
They would live in glory
And I would be ignored.
I am human just like you,
I contribute from a
Different point of view.

I've got wheels, you have feet.

They both do the same,

They make life sweet.

I've been traveling down this beach,

Trying to figure out

What these people preach about,

I thought they worshiped

Jesus Christ,

The one man that loves you

Whether you're wrong

Or you're right,

But the way you treat people like me,

I don't believe Jesus would do that, you see,

He believes in equal humanity.

He looks at everyone equally.

He looks at everyone equally.

One of the things that I regret sometimes is taking him to Texas in 2007. Don't get me wrong, I love my family and we truly wanted to have him be part of their lives.

Although our stay was short, he was able to do that and to visit the area where I was born and raised. They say that things happen for a reason, and I suppose losing my job in Texas and having to sell our beautiful "dream" home all happened for a reason. This next poem says it all regarding his feelings. This is an expression of the treatment of people with disabilities in that area of Texas.

The Devil's Mouth

>I've been living in the Lone Star State
>
>Most people are pretty nice,
>
>But some people are cold as ice
>
>I've been living in the 19th century
>
>I've been living in a 3rd World country.
>
>I guess it was my fate
>
>Moving to the Devil's State
>
>I sure cannot wait
>
>To move back to the Paradise State.

So many Republicans

They are everywhere

Wherever I roll, they are

Sitting right there

Religion, that's all they know

The "Good old boy" is the system they flow.

"Texas pride." that's what they say

To me it's just an excuse day after day

I guess it was my fate

Moving to the Devil's State.

I sure cannot wait

To move back to the Paradise State.

It's hot and humid

I'm nothing but human bait

Don't get me wrong

Texas is a great place

But since I've been here

I've had a frown on my face

> Friends and family, I miss you so much
>
> I can't wait to get back in touch
>
> I've been living in the Lone Star State.
>
> I guess it was my fate,
>
> Moving to the Devil's State.

As you can tell, Jeremy was not only our golden child but a very wise young man. He was very aware of the political climate at the time and always had an opinion about it.

When he talks about "I'm nothing but human bait," the following poem will clear that up.

The Mosquito Song

I've been living in South Texas,
One thing I hate the most,
It's not the humidity.
It's those damn mosquitoes.

They love to nibble on me
From my head down to my toes,
I don't know why,
And nobody really knows.

They're like little vampires
That fly in the day.
I try to avoid them
In any kind of way
I use "Off," it does no good.
I'd destroy each one if I could.
They love me so much
Because of my sweet blood,

They swarm around my body,

Like a great giant flood.

The environment here is really rough.

Take me back to Cali, so I can

Get away from this stuff.

We brought him back to Cali in the Spring of 2010. When I left in November 2009 for a new job in California, our goal was to get him back as soon as possible. It was very difficult to leave him in Texas with his dad being his only caregiver until we could sell our home and we could all be reunited. The following poem is his way of telling me, all was good.

Mother

Oh, Mother, don't you worry

Dad and I are just fine

We're hanging out at the house

Doing what guys do all the time

Drinking beers, watching movies,

Staying up all night
Going to the beaches
Building fences and
Fighting the good fight.

Oh, Mother, we miss
You so very much
There are four to our family,
But there are two of us.
The things that you do
To brighten up our day,
Dad and I will be bummed
Until you come back our way.

Oh, Mother, everything
Will be alright.
Dad and I will try
Not to dread at night.
You work yourself to death,
Each and every day.

To keep this family up

In a stable kind of way.

We're going through some

Tough times right now,

But Mother, don't you fret,

Don't you give me a frown

We'll make it through this as a family, as one

So, one day, we'll all be back in

Cali having some fun.

Jeremy was always aware of the reality of the world we lived in. His heart was full, and I am so sure that had he had a "normal" life in that had he not been born with a life-threatening disease, his contributions to the world would have been boundless.

I will add one more of his poems that he wrote as his "Best man speech" for his brother and new wife, Deidra on October 4, 2009. It goes like this…

Compassion

I've got something to tell you
About a man I know
He's a real swell guy
With a sweet afro.
I love him so much
And so proud of him
He just got married
To a beautiful woman

He's my brother
That Ian with an "I"
Yeah, he's my brother
He's always been by my side
Yeah, he's my brother
I'll love him 'til I die
We're just like two stars
Chillin' in the sky.

I just want you to know

I want you to understand

One reason I am here

It is because of you, man.

You already know

What I've been through

I would have never made it

If I didn't have a brother like you

You've gone out of your way

To make a sacrifice

And you are always there

When I need some advice

He's my brother

That's Ian with an "I"

Yeah, he's my brother

He's always been by my side

Yeah, he's my brother

I'll love him until I die

We're just two stars

Chillin' in the sky.

Now that you know

How much you mean to me

I would just like to welcome Deidra

To our family tree.

The minute I saw her

I knew she was the one.

My sister-in-law

For many years to come.

I wish you two love and happiness

For many years

And to Mr. and Mrs. Waggoner

CHEERS

The Waggoners at Ian's wedding.

Chapter 16
"Keep Moving Forward"

Our lives are full with one very important part missing. However, Wayne and I are still together, and we continue to deal with life without our "golden child." Our saving grace is that we have Ian, Deidra, and McKinsey. We will continue to move forward as Jeremy would want us to and not dwell so much on "What if" but "How do we keep moving forward?" I think Jeremy would be proud of us for that.

Our home is filled with memories, and I still have not gotten rid of all the "stuff" from his school years. Eventually, that time will come, and I don't look forward to it. I know it is all part of the healing process and it is difficult for a wound to heal when I keep pulling the scab off. Nonetheless, the beautiful memories and pictures will sustain our souls for a few more years. The picture below was taken almost a year before Jeremy passed. I was trying to get a picture for our Christmas card that year. McKinsey's second birthday was a few months away. Memories are priceless. I treasure every moment we were able to share with him.

Sweet dreams, my precious angel; until we see each other again, we miss you and we are so lucky to have had you in our lives. As he would say, "Hasta la vista, Madre!"

The last family photo before Jeremy passed.

Chapter 17
The End or The Beginning

The legacy continues through artwork. McKinsey carries that art gene. These are some of her drawings, done freehand by looking at a picture, just like her Uncle Jere.

McKinsey's freehand artwork.

Life Happens, Keep Moving Forward

The Olivarez children at Abel's funeral. We had lost Jimmy two years prior, and Rick was too ill to travel. Left to right, Esmeralda, Albino Jr, Della, Fidel, Marina, Dora, Ema, and Louie. Sitting: Virginia, Mary, and Eva.

Epilogue

In the tapestry of life, we are each woven with threads of resilience, strength, and courage. My journey, born from humble beginnings and marked by myriad challenges, has taught me invaluable lessons about the power of perseverance and the beauty of resilience. From the simplicity of a childhood on a farm without electricity to the complexities of serving in the US Air Force and navigating the corridors of healthcare as a registered nurse, I have witnessed firsthand the transformative potential of embracing life's trials as opportunities for growth. And in the face of unimaginable adversity, as I fought fiercely for my son's quality of life against the backdrop of Werdnig-Hoffmann Syndrome, I discovered reservoirs of strength within myself that I never knew existed.

Life happens, but in our response to its challenges we uncover the true depth of our character and the boundless capacity of the human spirit to rise above. I hope my story sparked a realization in your own heart that you are capable of great things that can make a difference in the lives of others.

May God bless the remainder of your journey as your life happens.

If you enjoyed this book, please consider leaving a positive review on online bookseller websites. This helps them rank the book higher for other readers to find. Thank you.

www.ingramcontent.com/pod-product-compliance
Lightning Source LLC
Chambersburg PA
CBHW070056080526
44586CB00013B/1081